THE HIDDEN CODES OF GOD

A JOURNEY TO THE UNKNOWN SECRETS AND
DIMENSIONS OF THE DIVINE AND THE ENERGY OF
LOVE

BY

Robert J. Newton, J.D., N.D

THE HIDDEN CODES OF GOD

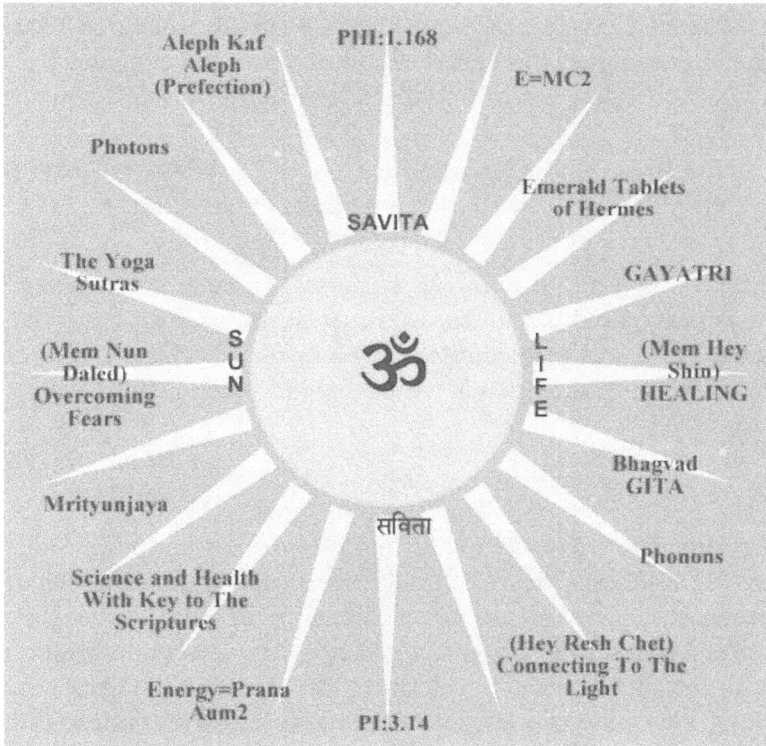

ADVANCE PRAISE

James' eye opening journey through *The Hidden Codes of God* is a conscious awakening for all of us... a healing... a must read.

~Scarlet Reynolds

Now I've read a lot of books in my life, but never have I gained so much knowledge and passion at the same time. *The Hidden Codes* is an easy read that keeps you captivated from the beginning to the end. I recommend this to anyone who wants to be free from the fairy tales of god passed down for generations.

~ Derek Dunlap
http://PositiveMarketer.com

I read this book in two days because I became so engrossed in James' incredible adventure through the realms of spiritual knowledge and romantic love. The book entertains you as it teaches you things that have been hidden from humanity at large!"

~ Bertha Nash

As I read this book, I could feel the passion and knowledge by which Robert wrote it. I have been studying many types of esoteric knowledge for more than four decades and I have never seen these concepts explained in such an interesting and insightful manner. Despite the complex subjects the book covers, it is enjoyable to read and easy to understand. How Robert did this I do not know but... do it he did. This is one book **everyone should read!**"

~ Charlette Ann Smith
Kriya Kundalini Yogini and Vedic Scholar

Once again, Dr. Newton has created a most compelling and fascinating book. *The Hidden Codes of God* sweeps you up in its current and carries you effortlessly through the entire story. For those people who have perceived there is more to know but have not yet found such, take heart, for it is contained in this book! *The Hidden Codes of God* can really help create a heaven on Earth, as it deals with spiritual and scientific knowledge that will transform planet Earth. The positive message of this book, in and of itself, will make you feel better about yourself and the future of planet Earth!

~ **Vaikunthanath Kaviraj**
Dr. of Homeopathy

Dr. Robert Newton has always given me credit for inspiring him to write, *A Map to Healing and Your Essential Divinity Through Theta Consciousness,* and that amazing book went into areas never covered by any book to date, even proving the existence of God as a controlling force in the Universe. With *The Hidden Codes of God*, he has surpassed himself with a most entertaining book dealing with spirituality and the scientific knowledge related to it, romance, and Divine Love. I became so entranced with this book I read it in one sitting as "The Hidden Codes of God" keep building into a crescendo. Each chapter supports and builds on the next one! Wow, what a special gem this book is!"

~ **Thomas Morton**
Founder, Light Speed Learning

"Francis Bacon very rightly said, 'Some books should be tasted, some devoured but only a few should be chewed and digested thoroughly.'

Dr. Robert Newton's book, *The Hidden Codes of God* is one such book, which requires the leisurely reading to relish it totally, and also grasp the message contained therein. From the very first chapter, there is the feeling that one is stepping into realms unknown, or to quote the writer, setting off on 'A

Journey to the Unknown Secrets and Dimensions of the Divine and Energy of Love.'

This book carries the essence of spirituality, no doubt, but there is a practical dimension added to it, which ought to attract not just the general readers, but also appeal to the young, modern readers who look for entertainment as well as substance that is grounded along scientific lines. That spirituality is not just a mystical concept is made clear to the readers in bits and pieces all throughout the book. Dr. Newton also points out in his book that one can aspire for perfection, even in this lifetime by aligning oneself with God through deep spiritual practices. In other words, he conveys the message that we human beings have been created in the image and likeness of God and ought to have been in that state of Perfection from the beginning, but our human follies and failings have destroyed this natural state and pushed us down lower the rungs of the human transformation ladder.

Dr. Newton also makes clear all is not lost as yet… because if we so desire, we can still restore things to their perfect state. To achieve this goal we will have to understand that Divine Love alone pervades the Universe and has the power to create the bonding through which all beings enjoy peace and bliss. The Divine is the source of all knowledge, and if we want to drink from the nectar from the source, we will have to train ourselves to become conduits through sincere spiritual practices. In a nutshell, the book explains to the seekers of spiritual knowledge how the human spirit can transcend matter and its various limitations ad directly connect with the Divine, even from the Earthly realm.

Oliver Wendell Holmes quote very beautifully sums up the essence of this book, "The best of a book is not just the thought which it contains, but the thoughts which it suggests; just as the chasm of music dwells not in the tones but in the echoes of our hearts."

~ Prof. Archana Bhattacharya
Indian Institute of Geomagnetism

Beyond the Bounds of Earth Publishing
Entertainment and Education

Dr. Robert J. Newton
20253 Evening Breeze Dr.
Walnut, California 91789
http://www.drrobertnewton.com/

Ordering Information:
Quantity sales. Special discounts are available on quantity purchases by corporations, associations, and others. For details, contact the publisher at the address above.
Printed in the United States of America

Great Motivational Talks
ISBN-13: 978-0996137102
ISBN-10: 0996137106
BISAC: Fiction / Alternative History

SECOND Edition
14 13 12 11 10 / 10 9 8 7 6 5 4 3 2

DEDICATION

This book is dedicated to those people with such an intense thirst to know and understand God they will overcome any obstacle put in their path of this pursuit. Always question everything; yet be pliable enough to accept new information that might be contrary to what you have already learned. At the very least, if you cannot understand something when it is presented to you, suspend judgment until you can ascertain the accuracy thereof. Also, never be reticent to ask for scientific and annotated proof of what someone presented to you, especially those who ask you to accept something on "blind belief." Additionally, know as certitude you can accomplish anything when you put your thoughts, energy, and powers of visualization toward accomplishing your goal. Live by this maxim, "The fool didn't know it couldn't be done, so it went ahead and did it anyway" (unknown). If you really want to get deeply into the concepts found throughout this book, check my other books including: *A Map to Healing and Your Essential Divinity Through Theta Consciousness, Pathways to God: Experiencing the Energies of the Living God in Your Everyday Life* and *Beyond the Mists of Time.*

Namaste, Dr. Newton

TABLE OF CONTENTS

ACKNOWLEDGEMENTS

Dr. Newton acknowledges the amazing teachers who helped him further his quest for spiritual knowledge and understanding of romantic and Divine Love. Those teachers include, John Alfred Clark, Edith Anderson, Mary Jane Heitzman, Julio Rivas, Mary Baker Eddy, Robert Chuck Schwartz, Charlette Ann Newton Smith, Dr. Paul Spin, Patrice Rybicki, Pamela Parvati Thomas, Yogi Govindan Satchidananda, Tim Latimer, Thomas Morton, William Sink, Babaji Nagaraj, Satchi Sai Baba, Amachi, Sri Aurobindo, Ghandi, Neem Karoli Baba, Paramahansa Yoganada, Yogi S.A.A. Ramaiah, Krishna, Yeshua (Jesus), Dr. Paul Foster Case, Hermes Trismegistus, Asclepias, Vianna Stibal, Louise L. Hay, Dr. James J. Hurtak, Dr. Wayne Dyer, Dr. Fred Bell, Ervin Lazlo, Rudolph Steiner, Ken Keyes, David Wilcock, Valery P. Kondratov, Gurudeva, Dr. Hugh Ross, Louis Contant, Dr. Rocco Erico, Rev. Richard Hill, and William Henry. Learn from these people in person, via their books, or their energy presence… you will rarely be misled!

CHAPTER 1

As a boy, James could never understand the ideas of his parents or for that matter, the ideas and ideals of society in general. While his parents had rules about the chores James was to perform around the house he lived in, this was less troublesome than the rules that he must keep his hair cut in the fashion of the day in the 1950's and 60's, even though he wanted his hair considerably longer. His father, George, would say, "James, I don't want you looking like a slob. Other people will judge the rest of the family by your appearance and you could embarrass us."

James protested, "You tell me that I need to get good grades in school and I do that. You also tell me that I must do my chores and I do them. How could the length of my hair possibly affect anyone but me? Why do you care what other people think? Why do their opinions even matter?"

His father said, "James, what you think does not matter! Anyway, there will be no shaggy dogs living in this house! You are not the head of the family— I am, not you and you do not have a say in this matter!"

In the fifties, this was the final word on most issues. Very few children had any say in any aspect of their lives, so James begrudgingly acceded to his father's demands. The consequences of disobeying his father were not worth fighting for the principles of his beliefs. Certainly, James would be spanked and sent to his room without dinner if he did not comply with his father's wishes

There were other things that really upset James, especially when he was between five and ten years old. He would have trouble sleeping at night because he could sense the presence of something or somebody in his room. This caused him to be very frightened, so much that he had great difficulty going to sleep at night. He could call his father or his mother, Martha, into his room and James would explain to them that there was something in his room. They would reply, "James, there is nothing in this room. Stop imagining things. There is nothing in your room!"

James would respond, "There is something here. Can I at least leave the light on in my room?"

His parents would return, "No James, just go to sleep right now! Stop bothering us about nothing!"

James thought, *why don't my parents believe me? I am sensing something in my room and nobody believes me! Am I really right about these things or am I just imagining things, as my parents are claiming?* It would take James thirty years until he began to understand about the ghosts and entities that kept him up at night. And it would also be about three decades before James would better understand these events that happen on astral dimensions. It would be a long and winding road on which James would travel!

James also could not believe how cruel his friends could be to people who talked a little differently or looked a little different from his other friends. He wondered why people would pick on other people about such small things that really did not matter when there were violent wars going on around the world. He could not understand the disparity between attentions to small problems in relation to real world crises. James was even more sensitive to these things because he was being teased about being a "freckle-faced freak" or his peers would say, because of the color of his red hair, "Better dead than red in the head!"

But the things that James found most problematic were the sermons he heard at the Baptist church, which his parents required him to attend. Even at five years of age, James found that the Sunday school teachers could not even remotely answer his questions about God. Yes, they spouted back answers to him that God was Love, but then he would hear the preacher at the Sunday morning sermon, tell him, actually yell at him and the congregation, that they were all going to hell and eternal damnation if they did not confess their sins and accept Jesus Christ as their Lord and savior. James was certainly scared by such ranting, but he still knew that the preacher did not understand much, if anything about God! *How could God be loving and at the same punish me*, James thought. What about the Sunday school teacher telling him that God was Love? James could not understand how a loving God would condemn him to hell if that God really loved him, no matter what perceived sins he had committed. If God would send him to hell for his un-confessed sins, James wondered how God could be Love and yet punish people.

Why was there no leeway in these matters? He did not know how he knew the pastor was misinformed about these things, but James was certain of his conclusion. It would take him about ten years to understand how he knew this, after he was exposed to Christian Science. The disparity between the loving God and the punishing God would take James at least a decade to start resolving, but he never stopped looking for answers to these things until he finally started getting answers that made real sense—not just arbitrary assertions.

When James' parents stopped going to church themselves, they still required him to go to Sunday school, but since the family had moved to another home further away from the Baptist church, they agreed that he could go to a Methodist church close to his home. At that church the confused young boy started finding partial answers to his questions about God and the suggested eternal punishment for unrepentant sinners. There was a kinder, gentler approach to these things and James appreciated the insights given to him by his Sunday school teacher, Bill. James enjoyed being around Bill and much preferred his nicer brand of Christianity. Yet, the issue of hell and eternal damnation of sinners was still embedded in the teachings.

James was entering his teens, and as often happens when we transit through puberty; James had strong emotional feelings for girls his age. Unfortunately, for him, he felt inferior to everyone else because of the constant kidding about his freckles and his red hair. There were several girls he found attractive, yet he was terrified to ask them out on a date. James wrestled with emotions of inadequacy as a person, even though he earned stellar grades in school, was a good all around athlete, had attained the rank of Eagle Scout within the Boy Scouts, and was an accomplished musician on the piano and the trumpet.

Often James was confused about everything within the societal structure. He felt there were too many arbitrary rules—rules, which were there only to suppress people rather the rules that really had meaning and purpose. He discussed these things with his father and mother, and despite their best efforts, he found their answers lacked the meaning and direction he required in his life. James thought, *if there is no real discernible reason or purpose to life, especially in regard to an angry God who needed to punish sinners who did not repent, what is the reason and purpose for living?* He was becoming confused and depressed because there seemed to be no one who could help him out of the dilemma.

Fortunately for James, intercession by one of his mother's friends would lead him to understanding God and bring purpose and meaning to his life. He was about to learn some things about "The Hidden Codes of God," although he would not understand the full significance of these revelatory codes until many years later!

CHAPTER 2

James' mother knew he was confused about life in general and the meaning of existence here on Earth. She was talking to her best friend, Sue, about the problems her son, James, was having and Sue suggested that James attend the Christian Science Sunday school at her Christian Science church. Martha, James' mother, relayed this message to her son. James was more than open to this idea but was rather surprised that his mother told him about this because she really did not have any deep religious tendencies.

When Sunday arrived, James was eagerly anticipating his visit to the Christian Science Sunday school. When he arrived, Sue was there to direct him to the Sunday school. She said, "I want to take you to Alfred's class. I think he will be the perfect teacher for you. In almost no time at all, James realized that he would be indebted to Sue for the rest of his life because the things that Alfred was telling James made complete sense to him even though he had never heard any of this before! Alfred was telling James that God had created the whole world and us in a state of perfection in his image and likeness.

James asked his teacher, "Where did you get this information?"

Alfred told him, "It is in *Science and Health with Key to the Scriptures*, by Mary Baker Eddy. She is the founder of Christian Science."

James then asked, "Why is there so much imperfection, sickness, greed and conflict among men?"

Alfred responded, "Mrs. Eddy says these things are nothing more than an illusion, that they must be an illusion because God created everything perfectly, in his image and likeness." The more Alfred explained Christian Science, the more James was becoming captivated by this religion.

James had never heard anything like this before, but the idea that man was created perfectly by his God really resonated with him. This certainly was very different from the ranting about sinners and hell from the Baptist minister. This particular Sunday was a day of real revelation for James; it was the beginning of understanding a validation that man was not a sinner condemned to the fiery recesses of Hell! He was glad that he had rejected the ideas of the ranting Baptist minister; otherwise, he might not have been open to this message of inherent perfection!

This day was likewise the beginning of a lifelong search for "The Hidden Codes of God." But it would be almost fifty years before James was able to put Christian Science, other spiritual teachings and scientific revelations into a book where this could be explained from a larger perspective, beyond that of Christian Science alone. On this pivotal day, James knew that from this point forward Christian Science would always influence him because immediately the meaning of life and existence was being revealed him. James thought, *why did not my parents know of these things? Why did so few other adults know and understand these things?* To answer his queries, like an overall understanding of the hidden codes, would take about fifty years to occur.

But James could care less about this long-term perspective. He could not wait to tell his parents about his new discovery and how it allowed him to be a happy person for the first time in many years. When James shared his new discovery with his mother, she said, "Fine dear, I am glad this is helping you!"

James then asked, "Do you want to learn more about this?

His mother responded, "No, dear, I am not as interested as you!"

Then James related his experience with Christian Science to his father who also indicated he really was not interested, leaving James to ponder, *Wow, this is almost incomprehensible, my parents disinterest in the revolutionary things I have learned!*

James next went to tell his best friend, Allen, about learning that we are perfect beings created by God. James though that he would surely be receptive to these ideas—that Allen was much more than he had been taught he was. James had a real rude awakening when Allen told him, "We are imperfect sinners that can only be saved by confessing our sins and accepting Jesus Christ as our Savior!

James, of course, protested, "Mrs. Eddy says that God created us perfectly as per the first chapter of Genesis in the beginning chapter in the Bible. Allen shook his head violently, back and forth, in disagreement. James was not dissuaded by Allen's inability to comprehend what he had just learned. Allen was a fundamentalist Christian and as James would find, throughout his life, they would rather remain as "saved sinners" rather than their inherent Divine and perfect beings.

James had by then purchased a copy of *Science and Health with Key to the Scriptures* from the Christian Science Church and instead of playing basketball he remained focused on studying his new book and learning everything in it. And that is just what he did, much to the chagrin of his parents, who always saw him participating in one sport or another in all of his free time! Also, James who frequently rode his bicycle or his skateboard was now more obsessed with absorbing as much information about "The Hidden Codes of God" as was humanly possible!

CHAPTER 3

James really devoured the contents of *Science and Health with Key to the Scriptures*. It took him two days to read about six hundred pages. Over and over again, Mrs. Eddy would explain that man and the Universe were not comprised of matter, this so-called dense thing that scientists, and especially physicists, were saying that all things were comprised of. James felt very liberated knowing that he was a perfect expression of God and that he did not have to be subject to sin, sickness, disease and death, as was repeatedly stated by Mrs. Eddy. His thoughts were filled with questions, *how did this woman figure out the science behind Christianity? Why did it take over eighteen centuries for this wonderful gift to be given to humanity? Why are so few people availing themselves to these wonderful teachings?"*

Mrs. Eddy said that the true message of Jesus was revealed to her after she almost died from an acute sickness of many months. She also said that she had studied the Bible incessantly and prayed constantly to be healed of her sickness and be given knowledge to understand herself and the world. In fact, Mrs. Eddy healed herself and led an extremely active life until she passed away! Mrs. Eddy never intended to create a new religion. Rather, she thought that the existing Christian churches would take her revelations and embrace them and accept a higher concept of Jesus and his teachings. However, Mrs. Eddy was rebuffed and labeled by virtually all theologians and clerics as a heretic!

James would soon experience the same type of treatment by many Christians, as did Mrs. Eddy. He was very enthusiastic to share what he learned with his friends and adults and he effusively spouted sayings and concepts from *Science and Health*.... Unfortunately, his enthusiasm was of no avail in persuading other people and friends to learn about Christian Science. To James, however, this did not matter because he knew that there were codes and information from God of the greatest importance for humanity and himself. James knew that these secrets of Jesus were divinely authorized as Mrs. Eddy claimed.

James was suddenly anxious to apply what he had just learned, in his everyday life. He was sure that he had found all the secrets of God, which he would use for the rest of his life. Eventually, he would learn that "The Hidden Codes of God" would be found in other places also. But the journey to that discovery would be an arduous and long process, with many experiences and some dead ends before it would be fully realized. But a most fascinating journey it would be, regardless of the obstacles encountered and many changes in direction along the way!

CHAPTER 4

James was anxious to apply what he had learned from *Science and Health*…. In fact, he already felt liberated from his depression because of Mrs. Eddy's perspectives from the Bible. This was a blessing beyond what he could have previously conceived. He certainly did not understand everything involved in this change in his outlook on life; he just knew he was ecstatic about all he had learned thus far and how it changed him. Of course, he had previously experienced fleeting happiness about his accomplishments and during sporting events or playing music, but the joy never lasted for any extended period of time.

About two years before he was introduced to Christian Science, James' mother took him to a psychiatrist who prescribed strong tranquilizers for his depression and his anger… the anger being the result of no one being able to give him answers about God or how to stay happy in life. James often thought of killing himself because life on this planet just seemed too difficult and unrewarding, despite his many impressive accomplishments.

While the tranquilizers calmed him, he really did not like the effect they had on him. It was like being half asleep and everything seemed to slow down. It was like being stuck in a frustrating dream. It was like living your life with about half of your previous energy. Finally, James convinced his mother to let him stop taking the tranquilizers.

Things in life went smoother with the tranquilizers but everything was boring— almost like sleeping. Although he was still depressed and angry, he actually felt better than with the sedatives.

With questions always rattling around in his mind James wondered whether he could apply the concepts of scientific Christianity to different aspects of his life. *Can I heal sickness? Can I learn things more easily and quicker? Can I do musical performances without getting nervous and shaking in fear? Could I talk to girls without getting nervous and not worry about being rejected if I ask them out on a date?*

The first thing James promised himself, was that he would have no more medical operations and surgical procedures for the rest of his life. He reasoned, *why should I have operations when I can heal my body?* The commitment was liberating to him although everyone else pretty much believed such thoughts were lunacy. James really did not care whether other people approved of his newfound belief or not. He knew it was considered an extremely radical perspective to heal yourself using prayer and knowing the true perfect essence of man.

The first thing James did was to heal himself of the frequent headaches he would get. Aspirin, the pain relief drug of the fifties and sixties, really did not work much to relieve his pain. Also, he used his knowledge of the Christian Science healing system to overcome a cold. Next he healed himself of dysentery without drugs. *Wow, James thought, not only do I feel better, but also I can actually heal myself.* So he told his friend, Allen, about the accomplishment, but found Allen really was not interested. And then James proceeded to tell several other friends who just laughed at him as well. To which James responded, "I know this is hard to believe but have I ever lied to you in the past?" Again, they laughed and just shook their heads in disbelief!

Again, James had to face that few people were ready to accept what he learned and that they would rather use doctors to heal them rather than their own efforts. The denial of others did not overly bother James as much his own inability to understand why people would not want God to heal them. Still, James kept plowing ahead in applying his new discovery. He realized that his study time and the retention of information and the writing of term papers was easier and more complete now that he completed them from the perspective of his intelligence coming from God rather than from his brain. The concept Mrs. Eddy used was that all intelligence comes from Divine Mind/God and that God is omniscient (all knowing) and that man links himself with this capacity as he acknowledges the relationship.

James term papers became easier to write and were better explained. His school tests were easier to take and his grades were even better. *Wow,* James thought, *why doesn't everyone use 'The Codes of God' in Christian Science to make their lives easier and better?*

Not too long after his introduction to Christian Science, James had a solo trumpet recital; he had performed previously, but he was always nervous before and during the recital and his arms shook so much that it affected his ability to play his trumpet at the level he knew he could. People would always tell him at the previous recitals, that they enjoyed what he played but James knew he was not performing up to his ability. By concentrating on knowing that he was connected to Divine Mind as his arms were connected to his body, James embraced this new recital… no longer nervous nor were his arms shaking. James could not believe how much better he played his trumpet and how much more an enjoyable experience.

James thoughts drifted to Sue, his mother's friend, who introduced him to this hidden knowledge of God contained in *Science and Health* and to his Sunday school teacher, Alfred, who had taught him so many useful and liberating things. He still did not have enough confidence to ask a girl out on a date, but he knew he would eventually. He had come so far in such a short period of time that he was grateful for how his life was changing for the better. James kept thinking, *things are so much better in my life I must be dreaming. Eventually I will find a way to share these things with other people. I don't know how now, but someday I will.*

And in fact this would happen—when James began writing his books, many decades later!

CHAPTER 5

APPLYING THE GOD CODES TO HIGH SCHOOL—
A REAL CHALLENGE

So things smoothed out for James in school until he started high school. All of a sudden there was a hierarchy like nothing he could have ever anticipated. The seniors and juniors were very aggressive to freshmen and sophomores. The goal was to avoid being hazed, being shoved around and insulted by the upper class mates. Most minutes James spent in high school were spent trying to evade being harassed in one manner or another.

The thought came to James that he could win these bullies over through using humor and trying to get on their good side. He thought of how Mrs. Eddy talked about how man, all men and women, were made in the image and likeness of God and therefore all of them reflect this perfection of the Creator. James also remembered how Mrs. Eddy talked about how fear created sickness and/or how it prevented healing from taking place. Reasoning this concept could apply equally well to human relations, James realized that if he changed his perception of these bullies, regardless of their disrespect and intimidation of him, things could change. What did he have to lose? Really, nothing!

Armed with a new perception of the situation and with the implementation of the campaign of humor, James was startled at the way his humor changed the way the upper classmen treated him. Much of his humor was directed at himself, which was very disarming to his antagonists.

Also, James found that complimenting the bullies about their clothes or their muscles or their intelligence improved his relationship with them. James' grandfather told him once, "If you respect people they will respect you, too." James thought that his grandfather obviously knew what he was talking about and so did Mrs. Eddy and his Sunday school teacher, Alfred.

It didn't take long before the word of James' humor became legend in his school. More and more people wanted to become his friend, leaving James thinking, *This is really hard to believe, considering everyone was pretty much avoiding me when I started school here.* James was becoming somewhat of a celebrity and soon, people were telling stories about him, with very exaggerated discussions of his antics. The funnier and goofier James acted, the more popular he became.

Soon, even girls started liking him and this was most fortuitous for James in that he gained confidence in talking with girls and with much more ease in doing so. Certainly, James really liked several girls in school, and finally, he got the courage to ask Ann, a girl he had known since grade school, out on a date. When he approached her, James had a smile on his face, as did she, and he said, "Would you consider going out on a date with a red headed freckle faced freak?"

Ann laughed, but quickly responded, "I really never ever noticed that your hair is red or that you have freckles. And I would like to have a date with you. What took you so long to ask me out?" "It was getting to the point where I thought I was going to have to ask you out, first." Ann told James, "I really like your smile and I really like your style."

James responded. "Oh, so you are attracted to funny guys, huh?" Ann said, "I sure am, but I dig your red hair, like big time!"

James then said, "I thought you said you did not notice my red hair."

Ann smiled as she said, "How the hell could I not notice your fiery red hair? There is something about you... kind of like a glow and a confidence, that makes you so attractive and your blue eyes just knock me out!"

So then James responds, matching her affectionate tone, "It is funny that you talked about that glow around me because to me you look like an angel. Your halo is so bright and sexy! You know when we used to dance together at Mrs. Putnam's dance classes, I always wanted to ask you out on a real date, but I was intimidated because you told me you were dating your older brother's friends!"

Ann gave James a wry look and with a twinkle in her eyes and said, "James I was only trying to make you jealous so you would think I was desirable enough to ask out on a date."

James felt the courage to respond further, "Well it had the opposite effect because it seemed you were making yourself unapproachable."

Ann's response rather surprised him, "Obviously, I screwed up and punished myself because I got the opposite result from what I wanted."

The conversation continued as James replied, "Ann I don't really care anymore because we will be together for at least one date and that makes me so damn happy!"

Ann winked and said, "James you are not going to get off the hook as easy as that. We will be having many, many dates in the future."

James just looked at Ann with a million dollar smile and said, "Wow!" and then fell to the ground. Ann said, "Why are you being so goofy?"

"I thought you liked goofy," James said.

"I do James; never stop being your goofy, joyous self," Ann said.

Not a moment lapsed before James returned, "Your wish is my command! Would you like me to fall on the ground again?"

"Sure," Ann said, "as long as you keep making me laugh and you come over here and kiss me."

"How about I hug you first and then give you a lot of kisses?" James queried.

"That will work for me… and then some," Ann responded.

CHAPTER 6

All the while James was kissing Ann he had the sensation electricity was passing between himself and her. It felt so incredibly good that James was delirious with delight. *How could this feel so good?* His teacher Alfred had no answers for him other than this is the "magic" that happens when a man and a woman connect with each other. "What did Mrs. Eddy say about this?" James asked Alfred. Alfred just replied, "Mrs. Eddy said we should avoid sensuality. She says it is an aspect of mortal mind and we should minimize these things our lives."

Suddenly James felt he might have to take a divergent path from Christian Science... at least on this issue. Yet he had no one or no source to explain these things to him; it would be another twenty-five years until James started to get a proper explanation about kissing and sexuality, even though he would enjoy them beyond any words he could ever use to explain!

When James next met Ann, he was so glad to see her again because they were going on their first date. The first thing he did when he saw her was to give in to his desire to give her a big hug. He lifted her off the ground and then he began kissing Ann rather forcefully. Ann said, "That is a little too rough of kissing to start out with, even though I love your kisses."

Not quite sure how to deal with all this newly found emotion James immediately apologized. "I am sorry,"

James responded. "I guess I got carried away. You just feel so good, Ann."

Ann felt it necessary to provide a little instruction and offered, "Sweet James, just start out soft and delicate and work up the intensity a little bit at a time. I will give you subtle hints so you can be sensitive to my needs."

Elated by her warm sensitivity, James replied, "That I can do! You make me feel so electrified and alive, like nothing I have ever experienced." "Do you feel what I am feeling?", James asked Ann.

"I do," Ann replied, "you are right, it is like electricity and it feels so amazing."

"I am glad you said that, Ann, because I thought I might be imagining things," James said.

James experienced another deep feeling of relief as Ann replied, "I doubt we are both hallucinating, James! Do you think we are?"

"No," James replied, "no way." "But when I asked my Sunday school teacher about this, he did not really say much except that it is based in sensuality and should be minimized in your life." Now, why on earth would I want to minimize something that energizes me like no other thing?"

Ann's response was rather a surprise, "I have no idea, what did your parents say, James?"

"They were basically evasive about it," James said. "What do your parents say about this Ann?"

"Pretty much like what your parents said, which was very little," Ann replied.

There was a momentary silence as James continued his confused pondering: *Why is everyone so hung up and uninformed about these things? If no one can even tell me why kissing feels so good, how much less will they be able to tell me about sex?*

Yes, they talked about babies and sex in sex education classes but no one mentioned the feelings that resulted from this. James realized that it might be a long time until he would understand just what occurred during the kissing between a man and a woman. Then James calmed down and realized he would figure things out eventually. *After all,* James thought, *I already know more about man, creation and God from a source that has largely been ignored and unknown—insider information from God.*

Even facing so many unanswered questions, James was looking forward to his date with Ann that night. "Hey James," Ann asked, "can we go to the drive-in movies tonight and get something to eat before we go."

"Yes," James replied. "Let's go to 'In and Out Burger' and then the drive-in theater. We better hurry though because it won't be long until dark and the movie will be starting."

While at the "In and Out," waiting for their food, James needed to know how Ann would look at his beliefs and felt compelled to ask her, "What do you think about my being a Christian Scientist? Are you okay with it?"

"Yes I am James, didn't you know my father was a Christian Scientist—and my grandfather too?" Ann responded. "It causes problems within our family because when my brother or I get sick, my mom wants us to go the doctor and our dad wants us to go to a Christian Science practitioner."

Needing to understand the depth of her own feelings on the matter James asked, "Where would you rather go, the doctor or the practitioner?"

James was holding his breath, but it didn't take Ann too long to respond. "Probably the practitioner. I like the idea that we were made perfectly in the image and likeness of God and that the natural state of man is health, since we have been created in God's image and likeness."

His next words just exploded from him as James exclaimed, "Damn! No wonder I like you so much. Not only do your kisses send me to higher realms, but you also understand the things that are important to me. Do you know how special that is, where two people get together and they just kind of blend together and really enjoy and adore each other?"

"Geez James," Ann responded, "I really do because my parents argue way too much, even though I know they love each other."

James then shared, "My parents get into nasty and really big arguments and they yell at each other. It is hard to call that love, from my perspective."

"I know," Ann said, "I think you are right. What is wrong with our parents? Let's just say that one of our four parents might know what is going on about these secrets of God that everyone should know. It sure would make their lives so much better.

Ann's comments prompted an intriguing question from James. "Why is there so much resistance to this truth?" It was more rhetorical in nature, and he immediately answered it, saying, "It just smooths things out so much.... just makes you feel better. This world will never change enough to attain its potential until its people accept and practice the underpinnings of perfection that pervade the Universe,"

Ann then said, "At least we have each other. I feel so much better when I am with you."

"You really know how to make a guy feel like a million dollars, Ann," James said as he was laughing and basking in Ann's joy-filled presence. "I wonder if there is more than these teachings of Christian Science?" James pondered out loud.

"I don't know," Ann replied, "but we should be grateful for what we already have."

It was a statement to which James easily agreed, saying, "That is what Mrs. Eddy says, that we should be grateful for what we have so that we can have more blessings come to us from God and I agree with you and then some. I am so stoked about everything!"

The sun had gone down and the movie was about to start by the time the couple, so engrossed in their conversation, finished eating found their way to the drive in movie. James went to the snack bar and got some popcorn and some Cokes for them to drink later. James said to Ann, "Do you think we will even see much of the movie?"

Not sure where her next comment would lead, Ann coyly replied, "James, "like, duh, everyone knows that lovers come to these passion pits to make-out and fondle each other!"

Relying on his successful attempts of humor, James queried, "Oh, they are drive-in passion pits—that is what they call them?"

Wanting the evening to be more than conversation Ann replied, "Too much talking, James, let's get cozy and whatever."

Whatever," James responded, "I like whatever!"

CHAPTER 7

After having a passionate night with Ann at the drive-in theater, James took her home, gave her several kisses and made sure she got into her house without any problems. After saying their goodnights, James drove home and started trying to figure out what happened when he was being intimate with his girlfriend. Many thoughts went through James' head as he was driving. *What actually occurred tonight? Was it a physical reaction or was it an energy or electricity that was being shared between us?*

The following morning, James went to the library and checked out a book on human sexuality. The book covered human erogenous zones, which included the lips, the neck, ears, the breasts, the vagina, the penis, the buttocks, the inside of the thighs and the feet. It conveyed that touching these areas elicits passion in men and women. James was still confused; the book never explained or described what this "passion" might actually be or where it comes from. "Could this be the 'Spirit' Mrs. Eddy talked about in *Science and Health…?"* What is Spirit, is it energy—electromagnetic energy?" One question following another, James heard each as he considered them out loud.

Knowing he had to find answers to these questions, James started asking his friends about them after he left the library. Besides being surprised at this serious question from their "funny man" they all thought he was on a futile quest.

"What difference does it make?" his friend, Allen, said, "We like what happens when we kiss and whatever and girls like what happens also. Why is it important, why do you need to know?"

Not to be dissuaded in his quest, James responded, "There is something going on when a man and a woman join together in passion. If we really understood it we would be better lovers!"

Then a thought came to James: *We really become relaxed when we are being passionate. I wonder if this was why I could feel electricity coursing throughout my body?* It would still be many years until James fully figured these things but he was happy with his revelation as he thought, *Relaxation leads to passion and passion elicits a lot of energy between a man and a woman.* What else would James learn in the upcoming days? He was very interested to know what it would be!

CHAPTER 8

James began to notice some interesting and unexpected things happening as he was trying to figure out how and why passion could lead to such incredible fields of energy in and about a person during the intimacy shared between a man and woman. These insights were coming to him without having studied or having previous knowledge about them. He asked Ann about it and she related that this was called, or considered something akin to, women's intuition. That wasn't answer enough, so James asked further, "But what is this actually?"

Ann responded, "It is like a premonition, which is knowledge that something will occur before it actually does. Do you see the similarity, James?"

James replied, "Yeah, I am getting a feeling for it. But no one has yet been able to explain just how either of these things do occur. Why is there so little information about something that helps us so much?" Ann really did not have any more answers to James' questions, so he asked Alfred, his Sunday school teacher, knowing he would get nothing from his father or mother.

Alfred told James, "Such information comes from God or Divine Mind, as Mrs. Eddy related in *Science and Health*.... Alfred further explained, "God is omniscient, which is all knowing."

was quiet for a moment, and added another comment, "As we align ourselves with God through prayer, we ultimately become conduits through which divine knowledge is related to us."

But then James had another thought to himself, *I really was not in prayer when I got this knowledge.* But he realized, when he was in a state where he was quiet and still, he also remembered how Mrs. Eddy talked about "listening to the still small voice within," as a way to connect with God and his knowledge. In fact, Mrs. Eddy even related in other of her works how she used this practice to uncover the science of Christianity.

James further remembered that Mrs. Eddy said that we should all live in a state of constant prayer. So then James surmised that he too might be entering a state of constant prayer to uncover insights and inspiration about things to which he had no previous knowledge. A couple of decades later, James would learn that these thoughts and feelings are called intuition and sometimes, Akashic knowledge, which is basically considered knowledge from the heavens.

James then somehow got the idea that he could use this connection to God to know what people were thinking without any type of verbal communication. The next time he met Ann, he tried if out! When he met her, he did not say anything but rather concentrated on trying to figure out what she was thinking and how she was feeling.

Ann broke the silence and asked James, "Why are you being so quiet? It is kind of weird."

She was surprised by James' reply. "I am trying to read your mind. I know you are upset because your parents just had another one of their arguments. And I know you are sad and a little depressed about the whole thing."

Ann responded, "Wow, James you are so right about both of these things. How did you figure that out?"

It didn't take long for James to reply, "I used Divine Mind and my connection to it."

Remembering their earlier conversation, Ann replied, "Oh, you mean women's intuition?"

James was solemn as he answered, "Yeah, sort of like that but I think all of this information comes from God. I am proving right now that men can have these insights as well as women! What do you think about that?"

A small smile broke through her lips; "Well," Ann responded, "I know you don't kiss like a woman so you must be a man and you must be right. When are you going to teach me to do this?"

Their banter continued as James replied, "I don't know if it can be taught. Anyway, I know you are woman because you don't kiss like a man and so you should already know how to do this!"

Moving beyond the humorous side of James she enjoyed so much, Ann said, "You know, you are right James. I can and do the things you were doing—figuring out what people are thinking. I do it all the time, but I did not think of it as anything that is special. I just kind of know what people are thinking—just knowing without thinking about it."

Delving deeper into the conversation, James said, "You know Ann, "I think Mrs. Eddy thought these things were and are possible for all humans to perform—to know. Wow, we are kind of sneaky smart about these things, Ann."

"Yeah, sneaky smart and then some. But just whom are we going to talk to about this? Really? Certainly not our parents or any of our friends, are we James?"

"You got that right!" People think I am weird already; why would I want to confirm their suspicions? These abilities are hidden codes of information from our Creator and are hidden from people because they never seek out this information or think they are incapable of such!"

James just hoped that someday, somewhere, people would have a thirst for the knowledge and concepts he had learned.

CHAPTER 9

In senior Social Studies class, Mr. Noyton gave an assignment for a 5 to 10-page term paper about how to properly dispose of the trash we generate in our society. James, being a part of the class, thought it would be quite a difficult undertaking, since neither government nor private enterprise was doing much about the problem except either to burn the trash or bury it. This was the modus operandi of the sixties and it was 1964. James knew it was idiocy just to burn or bury trash. At this time, the concept of recycling things was unheard of, except for the deposits for soft drink and beer bottles. When returned to a grocery or liquor store, the money for the deposit was refunded and the same bottles would be cleaned and reused, over and over.

So, as James was kind of daydreaming one day, not far from the date his term paper was due, the idea came to him that everything should be recycled. In current day and time, the idea is self-evident, but back then it was never discussed or considered, except for bottle deposits. Wow! James thought, *how did I ever get this idea?"* Reminded of the concept of intuition, one of "The Hidden Codes of God," he knew exactly where the idea came from. James was learning that he could be a problem solver, which gave him confidence he would use it in the future to apply to many other situations.

James then embarked upon the writing of his term paper. Yes, he wrote about recycling and reusing all trash, including green waste, which could be made into compost, which would improve the growing properties of soil; green waste could also be converted into mulch, which could be used to conserve water in the soil and to prevent weed intrusion on soils. However, what really made James' paper something to think about was expanding his idea about the ultimate consequences to the environment if recycling did not become the mode of society.

James wrote about the idea that we could bury our trash in pits that were lined with plastic so that the trash would not leak into the water table and aquifers. This eventually came to pass and continues today in landfills. Then, he addressed how this burying could not be done endlessly since eventually we will run out of room to do so, or if there is room, it would be located in remote areas and would cost more and more in transportation expenses for disposal. Then James focused on what would happen if there were a large earthquake, which would tear the pit liner and allow trash and harmful liquids to leak into the water table… and how it would have long-term consequences that would be very detrimental to us.

Finally, James finished his paper and turned it into Mr. Noyton, feeling confident that he had done a good job in meeting the requirements for the paper. Several days later, Mr. Noyton had finished scoring the papers and everyone except James had their graded paper returned to them. As the teacher handed the papers back, James wondered what was going on. Then Mr. Noyton announced, "I want to read you one of the papers that is from one of your classmates! It is really quite amazing and solves a lot of problems we are now facing." As the teacher read his paper to the class, James felt really happy his teacher recognized his innovative work. James felt really proud of his accomplishment and yet he realized that the paper was "beyond him" and felt so grateful for all the things he ad learned from "The Hidden Codes of God" via the Science of Christianity.

Ann, who was in James' class, came up to him at the end of class and said, "James I am so proud of you. I knew you were smart and sweet, but now you are taking things to a higher level!"

As he was hugging and kissing and squeezing Ann, he said, "You know that while I wrote the paper the ideas came to me kind of out of the blue, convincing me I was divinely inspired… just as Mrs. Eddy talks about in *Science and Health*….

"You know, James," Ann replied, "if you can repeat what you just did with that term paper, you are almost an unlimited problem solver and then some."

"I know, James said." Yet look at how few people actually know this… you know, these secret codes. I guess someday I will have to write a book about it."

"Why don't you start writing a book now, James? There was pride in Ann's voice as she asked the question.

James replied, "Thank you so much for your confidence in me, my love, but I am not ready to do take that step; somehow I know I need to learn or discover more of these "secrets." But I will write it someday, I guarantee it!"

CHAPTER 10

James enjoyed just about all sports except soccer. He liked football, he loved basketball and he treasured baseball. But these are team sports and it was the individual sports that he really liked, which included were cross-country running and track distance running. His appreciation for individual sports was because not only did he not have to worry about interacting with his teammates, he could kind of exist in "his own world." James did not really understand the "own world" concept, but he knew that some unexplained things happened therein.

When James and the other runners did their practice runs during the week, in preparation for competition in cross country, it was not uncommon to run for ten or fifteen miles per day. At the beginning of the run, and maybe into the middle, it would seem to require a lot of effort to keep running. One thing that made this easier was running in a pack and not wanting to be the only laggard in the group. This seemed to keep everyone going.

But James soon noticed that after a certain period of time, all of a sudden it took very little effort for him to run. There was less exertion required and it seemed like he was entering a state of euphoria—really feeling quite incredible, kind of a like a state of transcendence beyond actually being completely present on Earth. James talked to the other runners on his cross-country team and they all agreed that after a certain period of time, maybe after three or five miles of running, running became very easy and enjoyable. So, seeing that this was something that most of the other runners were experiencing, James mind had him on to another query *Is this another of those "Hidden codes of God," that is manifesting itself in a mysterious, yet consistent manner?*

Mrs. Eddy spoke of the Bible passage, in *Science and Health*… "They shall run as with wings and they will not tire." And James' mind was once again the virtual storehouse of questions and answers. *Is this what we are doing? Are we entering this state of Spirit, transcending matter, that Mrs. Eddy talked about?"* James deeply wanted to discuss this subject with his teammates, but by this time he was fully convinced that few people were ready to talk about, let alone understand, "The Hidden Codes of God." Talking out loud James considered, "I could talk to Ann about this, even though she is not a runner. She is a cheerleader though and maybe she will understand it. And… maybe Alfred, my Sunday school teacher likewise knows about the idea."

Well, when he saw Alfred at Sunday school, he asked Alfred, who told James in no uncertain terms, "Although I am not a runner, like you, I can tell you that Mrs. Eddy told us that it was possible to live in a 'state of heaven on Earth.' Most likely you are entering heaven, even if it is only for a short period of time. She also said we need to transcend this state of matter and its various limitations. You might also be entering a state of prayer or meditation where you are actually able to directly connect with God."

Wow, James thought, *these are really powerful insights that Alfred has given me. These things make sense to me.*

James wanted to validate these new beliefs, and when he met Ann, later in the day, for a Sunday afternoon date, the first thing he asked Ann was, "Do you know what Alfred told me about running?"

"No," Ann replied, "but if you don't start kissing me real soon, I am going to have to find a new boyfriend, comprende?"

Ann laughed as James countered, "Wow, what an idiot I have been. I was so excited about what I learned I forgot to take care of my main squeeze. You can flog me with a wet noodle after I am done kissing and caressing you. Maybe if I kiss you long enough and passionately too, you will forget about my flogging!"

Breaking her laughter, Ann said, "Yeah, I will consider that, but you better put up or shut up, like yesterday!"

Now it was James' turn to be amused, and quipped, "OK, I am at your disposal, my princess," as he put his arms around Ann's waist and began to kiss in the sensitive and passionate manner she had taught him.

"Yes, James, that's just the way I like it. You are a quick and passionate learner."

"Thank you for noticing," James replied, "and also not only for appreciating me but for being the best of best friends too."

After spending a good amount of time in each other's embrace, enjoying the amorous mood, and feeling good about everything, James started telling Ann about what Alfred said about running. He asked Ann if this might also apply to cheerleading. So, Ann related how something did happen, but not exactly in the same way as running. Ann said, "We are not continuously moving like you are in distance running, but we do feed off the crowd. If we get a lot of participation in our cheers from the audience, then we get energized and cheerleading gets easier, a lot more enjoyable, and a lot less like work or effort."

"So, James… now when you are in the stands, I don't want hear any more of your half hearted, half baked cheers. I need your support so I can perform better and I know you have a loud voice so don't give me any lame ass excuses!"

"I understand now," James said, "I shall worship and support my princess."

"Thank you," Ann said laughing; "At least you respect my royalty."

"Well I do," James replied. "You are a real royal beauty and so damn 'schweet' too."

Ann said in a surprised manner, "where did you get that 'schweet' word from?"

A lover of questions himself, James replied, "I kind of made it up. It probably means you are sweeter than sweet. No man on this planet could be more blessed than to have you as his girlfriend." Ann just smiled approvingly and nodded, and looked at James with admiration and appreciation.

James was really glad he had created Ann to be a bigger presence in his life, but he knew from studying the hidden codes that he was in fact responsible for everything that happened in his life! He wondered what his next creation would be? In fact, James' friend from Boy Scouts, Ernie, would shortly introduce him to surfing. James had never thought a lot about surfing, but for some reason he was completely open to the idea. It could have had to do with the fact that James immensely enjoyed riding waves with air mattresses at the beach during the summers when he was growing up. He spent hours enjoying the sport and it was hard to get him out of the water.

One day, during Christmas vacation from high school, Ernie set up a surfing trip with one of James' friends, Jeff, and one of Ernie's friends, Wayne. They rented some surfboards in Huntington Beach and headed to Tin Can Beach. The wind was blowing quite hard, the water was cold, and none of them had wetsuits. But all of the boys took turns riding waves in quite marginal conditions, wave-wise. But when James stood up on his first wave and several others that followed, he knew he was hooked on surfing. There was a lot of shivering on the beach and some wave-riding going on, but eventually James' friends wanted to get out of the wind and cold and get something to eat. James protested saying, "It is not really that cold. Let me catch some more waves, and then we will go." James caught several more waves, but finally agreed to leave because the water was getting choppier and choppier; the waves were knocked down by the increasing winds.

But for sure, all James thought about was going surfing again as soon as possible. To him surfing was like being in another world. It was like being detached from the world and there was a feeling of freedom and euphoria that James heretofore had never experienced. In fact, it would be a considerable period of time—several decades—before James really understood what happened to him while surfing, but he knew immediately it would contain hidden codes. That understanding gave James a good feeling because discovering more aspects of the codes was his mission in life! The fact that almost no other people were interested in this was irrelevant to James because he had this unspoken, intuitive knowing that this was the right thing for him to do and manifested a higher purpose for his life!

CHAPTER 11

It was on the eve of prom night at James' and Ann's senior prom, but James was not exactly enthusiastic about attending this event. James knew that Ann was excited about the prom, as were her friends. It was not that James was not excited about spending time with Ann; rather it was that he really did not like formal events and also having teachers present as chaperones. Nevertheless, James agreed to prom pre-requisites: rented a tuxedo and bought Ann a corsage.

When James picked up Ann in his car, she was very happy with the orchid corsage and James was very happy with the beauty of Ann's dress. And yet, Ann could sense that James was less than thrilled about actually going to the prom. She asked him, "James, am I detecting you really are not into this prom thing?"

"You are right," he responded, "I really am not, but know that I am into you and you look so beautiful and radiant and that it is already making it easier for me to take you to the prom. When you are happy, I am happy likewise and so we kind of are feeding off of each other, right?"

"Yes, James," Ann said, and I bet you we will become happier as the night progresses. Just relax and enjoy being with me and you will see some magic happen."

"What kind of magic Ann?" James queried.

Ann replied, "Energy magic, like that Spirit magic from those hidden codes we are always talking about!"

"Well, James replied, now you are talking my language, I think. Are you talking about the energy of love?"

Ann responded, "Yes, that and more since everything is energy, which includes love. Isn't that what we have been talking about every since we became a couple?"

James smiled and then started laughing and nodded his head in agreement. "I can see that you intend to teach me something tonight," James said to Ann.

"Experience and learn!" Ann said as she smiled and winked at James.

When they arrived at the prom, which was held in their high school gymnasium, Ann told James, "Just concentrate on me and I will concentrate on you and we will take ourselves into another dimension as we are dancing with each other. Relax as much as you can and we will create an energy field, infused with love and it will be special just for us since no one else here could even conceive of this other than ourselves!"

Kind of at a loss for words, James replied, "Wow! You never cease to amaze me with your far out ideas that are so creative."

Ann responded, "I need to keep you interested and keep you captivated and I will do just that!"

When the couple got inside the gym, because of their mindset and because they were already very relaxed, the prom felt as though there was a very little electricity coursing throughout the building and into their bodies. As the band began to play a slow song, James took Ann by the arm and guided her onto the dance floor. He put his hand around Ann's waist and took her right hand, and as she took his left hand and put her left hand on his right shoulder, together they ascended into a euphoric state of consciousness! Soon, James had his other arm around Ann's waist and they melded into each other with a passionate embrace. The more they relaxed the happier and the more passionate they became. The energy they were creating became self-perpetuating and creating waves of ecstasy they could literally feel... a warm and tingling, electrical sensation.

The "electrical happenings: began even before James started kissing Ann passionately on her neck. And as Ann responded to these kisses, James began to tenderly kiss her lips with soft short kisses—followed by longer drawn ones — then repeating the sequence over and over.

Unbeknownst to James or Ann, the teacher chaperones were less than thrilled with their display of affection, but even if they were aware of this the two would not have cared in the least. Ann asked James, "What do you think is occurring to us? It is just so magical, you know."

And James replied, "You predicted it, my sweet love, that something magic would happen. Are you sure you are not a psychic?"

"Psychic, schimyic," Ann said, "I don't really care, but this feeling inside of me is really way beyond normal and so divine."

"Baby," James cooed, "I only wish our parents could feel what we are feeling and they would have no need to argue with each other, ever again." Ann just looked at James with deep passion filling her eyes and nodded in agreement.

After several slow dances, the band began to play a rock and roll song with a fast paced beat. James wanted to leave the dance floor until another slow song was played, but Ann convinced him they should continue dancing. James was glad she convinced him to do so because to his great surprise, the special energy that he and Ann had generated continued to build, much to James' astonishment. James was under the impression that if they were not dancing closely together, the energy and passion would dissipate. Although James and Ann both liked the faster dance, because it allowed a more creative dance expression, they did not expect the energy to keep building as it did. It seemed that they were able to keep and amplify the energy and passion just being in a close approximation without actually touching.

"James, you know that I am so energized and so turned on you could pretty much do whatever you wanted to do to me. Do you understand what I am telling you?" Ann asked.

James nodded and said, "I do and I would like to capture this moment and never leave it because it is just so ecstatic. I am so glad we came to prom and listened to what you wanted me to do—to relax. Truly, your value to me is beyond any amount of compensation conceivable. I think I understand now why and how so many babies are conceived in this state of hyper passion!"

46

Surprised at James' statement, Ann asked, "Why are you talking about babies, James? Do you want to make a baby with me?"

James responded, "No baby, I do not want to make babies with you, although right now I think I love you beyond anything I can put into words. But I sure as hell can feel it and I sure as hell can feel you too!"

"I feel, you too, Sweet James, and I want this to continue for a real long time, too!"

James replied, "Let it be so! I am sure this is part of 'The Hidden Codes of God,' but I am also sure that very few people will agree with me."

"Well then, James," Ann responded, "I will be your disciple for this!"

"Look at the other couples," James replied, "I am sure that some of them might be our disciples, too. I see a lot of amorous looks and a lot of affection going on here."

"Why are you looking at them," Ann queried, "I thought we were only going to have eyes for each other?"

"Oh baby," James replied, "do not be jealous. There is no one here whose aura radiates like yours. You are my shining star."

Ann then grabbed James around the neck and started kissing him passionately, with flurries of short kisses and then longer, more ardent ones and then put her tongue into his mouth and made contact with his tongue. James responded in like fashion and was amazed at how much passion could be elicited via "French" tongue kissing!

What a wonderful erogenous device for eliciting passion, James thought. *I wonder why this was not considered an erogenous zone in that book I checked out from the library about sexuality.*

CHAPTER 12

After the Prom was over, even though it was close to midnight, James and Ann went to a restaurant to have something to eat. They were basking in the tremendous energy created between them and had trouble letting go of each other long enough to even take a bite of food! What they wound up doing was feeding each other, in between their caressing. An older couple, about the age of their parents, came up to their table and commented on how much they seemed to be in love. James told them that they were basking in the energy of love, and the couple asked him what he meant by that.

James explained how Ann had proposed that they both become relaxed as possible when they arrived at the prom and that something special would occur from this. James told them, "I was quite skeptical about Ann's idea, but I agreed to go along with it anyway."

Ann then took over to further explain to the couple, "The tremendous amount of energy that began to be created from our experiment in relaxation was beyond anything we could have imagined. James and I already felt very special about each other before the prom, but at the prom, somehow our feelings for each other were magnified beyond what we could comprehend."

Then Ann continued in a very frank fashion while she explained, "By relaxing, the presence of God could enter into our bodies in a less impeded fashion and we could really feel the difference."

James then added, "I agree with everything that Ann has just explained and that we learned these things are part of 'The Hidden Codes of God.'"

The couple that had come over to their table looked somewhat incredulous about what James and Ann told them. Then each said almost simultaneously, "You kids been smoking some of that weed? Because that sounds kind of weird."

Ann replied even before James could say anything," No, we don't smoke Marijuana and the weird things we are telling you actually work. A lot of this stuff is in *Science and Health with Key to the Scriptures* and we both feel that there are 'Hidden Codes of God' in this book by Mary Baker Eddy!"

Then the couple responded, "Ok kids, maybe we have misjudged your comments."

James replied, "We are not offended because we are used to people telling us that we are weird or that we are crazy. Neither Ann nor I were very happy before we started learning about these things, right Ann? If you guys try this, technique, it will reignite the passion that may have left your relationship, even without having sex. You will be so excited and happy with this simple concept of relaxation it just might blow your mind like it did for us."

Ann then replied, "Everything he just said I agree with. May both of you be so blessed as us to have this occur in your life. This is our gift to you."

James then added as he was laughing. "If you want to pay for our dinner we would let you, you know." And then both nodded in agreement as the man plunked down some money on the table. But James said, "Oh, I was just kidding, we were not really soliciting money from you. I was just kidding, man!"

But the couple refused to take the money back saying, "You deserve it kids! You woke us up and we really appreciate that. Also, you did not get insulted when we called you weird. We think we need to be more like you and less like us!"

"We really appreciate that," Ann said, "and we hope we helped you!"

"Right on," James added.

The generous man added, "We normally never listen to teenagers, but you guys have something so special, it is like you are lighting up the room. It is like you have melded into one unit."

James then said, "As we relax more, the energy or inspiration of God can more fully pour into us and it is expressed as love… and the more we have, the more we can share… and the more we share, even more energy is created until it is like we are so filled it creates ecstasy and euphoria and you just feel so unexplainably good. Mrs. Eddy talks about many of these things in *Science and Health*…. but she does not relate them in the terms of romance, which she considers sensuality and to be avoided. But we believe we have discovered secret things that should not be secret and should be shared with everyone who will listen, which is not very many people right now."

"Whatever you guys are eating we want to eat too," the woman said. "Can we join you for a bite of food?"

"Sure," Ann said, "we just wish our parents would listen to us like you guys did and eat what we are eating so they can become crazy like us!" The couple, Ann, and James all laughed at what Ann had just uttered.

CHAPTER 13

After finishing their food with the couple at the restaurant, James asked Ann if she wanted to take things to the next level in their romance. Ann was open to this as she replied, "Remember I told you that you could pretty much do anything with me while we were at the prom and I was not just telling you that for my information only." "Yes Ann," James responded, "I very well remember you telling me that and it made me so stoked that you would feel that way about me. Would you like to go to the beach and dance in the moonlight or get a motel room?"

"Why don't we dance in the moonlight on the beach and then get a motel room down there?" Ann replied.

"Then both it is!" James responded. "Let's get in my Chevy and drive it to the levy or jetty and head down to Newport Beach and the Newport Pier." Ann just smiled and laughed at James' attempt at saying clever things.

When they arrived at the pier, the light of the full moon was reflecting off the water in a surreal fashion, like being in a magical place. James and Ann got out of the car and walked down to the beach as James put his arm very firmly around her waist. They arrived at the ocean's edge, just where the waves were crashing on the shore, James had his right arm around Ann's waist, took her right hand with his left and began to dance in a waltz like fashion, circling around down the shoreline.

"Good God," Ann said, "that energy we created at the prom is coming on even stronger, isn't it James?"

"I would have to agree with you and then some," James replied, "this is so far out—so beyond even what we created earlier in the evening. I can feel streams of electricity flowing between our hands and wherever our bodies are touching. When I kiss you it is like my head becomes so full of electricity that it literally changes my perception of things. It is like we are more spirit or energy than we are flesh. There is a stream of electricity coursing down my spine and into my head and circulating up and down"

"Well," Ann replied, "I remember you talking about how Mary Baker Eddy said that matter is an illusion and that we are spirit. I guess we are literally proving that right now because I agree with the effects that you have described. I wonder why we don't feel like this all the time."

James then said, "I guess we are not relaxed enough most of the time because we are stressed out and worried about so many things. This might show we are living in the future and creating problems for ourselves that many times would not have to happen in our lives. I am pretty sure we are uncovering and better understanding these hidden codes and knowledge of God. I know our friends will think this is crazy"

James and Ann danced for at least a half an hour with the energy between them increasing incrementally and with them becoming more and more delirious with ecstatic feelings. It was as if time no longer existed! Finally, James took Ann by the hand and said, "Do you think it is time to get a hotel room, Ann?" She nodded yes and smiled at him so sublimely that James thought he might be hallucinating. Yet he knew he wasn't imagining things, but rather seeing things with a different perspective. As they walked to the motel, close to the pier, James and Ann were both anticipating the passionate moments they would be sharing. It was like they were little kids at a birthday party who had just been given cake, ice cream, candy and pie altogether for dessert.

After James booked the room, they sauntered in that direction and as James opened the door, Ann grabbed his hand, yanked his arm and pulled him onto the bed with her. James went back to the door, closed and locked it and he leaped back to the bed. "Wow," James said, "you are so good to me, Ann."

And then Ann said, "And you are so good to me and good begets more good."

"Groovy," James responded, "but I would rather caress you than talk and that is just what I am going to do."

James and Ann were already both so high from kissing and caressing each other that they both doubted that that they could become any more amorous, although they hoped and anticipated that they would create an even more wondrous field of energy between and around them. James removed Ann's sweater and began to fondle her breasts. Ann smiled and writhed about and slightly sighed and moaned as he caressed them. James' penis became harder and harder as he gave his attention to Ann, and she emitted increasingly more intense sounds. James kissed Ann's neck and began to bite it. And she began to do the same thing to James, and she could tell that he was becoming very excited and more and more intense in his energies. While James tended Ann's breasts, she likewise began to fondle his. James rubbed Ann's tailbone, exciting her even more.

James then stroked the inside of Ann's thighs after he removed her prom dress; she removed his shirt and pants and they both threw off their shoes. As James stroked Ann's inner thighs she began to quiver with delight. It felt so titillating and she began throwing caution to the wind. She was kissing James all over his body in a frenzied and passionate manner. James then removed Ann's panty hose and began sucking on her toes and caressing her feet.

"Holy Jesus," Ann yelled out, "you are driving me out of my mind, James. Where did you ever learn this feet thing?"

"You know I am an avid reader," James said, "and after our first date I went to the library and checked out a book on human sexuality and I learned a lot of cool things like this and stroking your inner thighs and kissing and biting your neck. The other stuff everybody knows but I want to know more and perform better than anyone else. You know how fanatic I am about being the best at everything. And this is just another example of that."

"I do not have a condom," James told Ann, "and I don't' want to be making a baby, but I am going to make you feel so damn high that you will do anything I ask of you."

"I will," Ann replied, "if you can actually pull that off because I was so looking forward to having your penis stuffed into my vagina."

James quickly responded, "I was not going to put my penis in your pussy tonight, but I do not want to disappoint the woman who has helped me to change my life so much. So

I will penetrate your vagina with my penis, but I am not going to ejaculate inside of you. When things start getting close to a climax, I am going to withdraw from you and I will finish you off in another way."

As James entered Ann's vagina, he felt like he could hardly tell where his body began and where her body ended; Ann was experiencing the same things. They both thought that this aspect of oneness with each other was way too freaky, but the union between them could not be denied by either of them. The more that they let go of themselves, the more intense was the energy and pleasure that surrounded them. They had their arms tightly wrapped around each other so that they were lost in the energy of each other.

James felt like his penis was getting close to exploding, so he quickly withdrew from Ann and quickly moved his head down to her pubic hairs and inserted his tongue into her vagina. The smell of Ann's vagina was rather strange yet James was intoxicated by it and enjoyed it. James was flicking his tongue around the inside of Ann's vagina but then he remembered that most women needed their clitoris stimulated to achieve an orgasm. James did not exactly know how to locate the clitoris so he directed Ann to tell him when he stimulated her in a very intense manner.

Ann told him that she would give him a blowjob while he was taking care of her. But he declined because he wanted to make sure he did not orgasm before her. After some probing with his tongue, Ann began telling James, "You have hit the spot. Please, James, do not stop. Please drive me crazy, I beg you."

James replied, "You do not have to beg. I am going to love the shit out of you." And he proceeded to do just that, flicking his tongue on and around Ann's clitoris. She began climaxing and moaning and yelling and telling James how much she loved him and how they should be together for this and all other lifetimes they might experience together. James agreed that things could not get better between them.

But when Ann put his penis in her mouth and began rubbing his testicles and sucking his penis, he then realized that things could get better. It did not take James much time to shoot his load since he was already higher than any kite that he had ever flown. When James had his orgasm, he was yelling and writhing about like a fish out of water. "Geez Ann," James said, you transported me to another world."

And then Ann replied, "You did the same thing to me. There is energy in your sperm, although it tastes rather strange, it is energizing my whole being. My body feels very different and unencumbered by the limitations of matter!"

"Yeah," James said, "I think we have just discovered our true essence as spirit, energy bodies, which may just be the essence of the hidden codes!"

"Now, how do we do this all of the time? Let's see if we can figure this out in the afterglow of our energy explosions and the resulting energy field we created… or at least borrowed from the Creator!" James exclaimed.

▍CHAPTER 14

Basking in the tremendous amount of energy they
created together, James and Ann were relaxed in a
way that they had never experienced in their entire
lives. In the condition of extreme energy, with which they had
created and surrounded themselves, describing it in words
was virtually impossible because there were no words of
reference that applied to the feeling except euphoric and
ecstatic. No one would understand, unless they, too, had
achieved the sexual energy creation that James and Ann were
expressing. Words were abstract and totally inadequate to
express their state of consciousness.

"I am seeing things like there is a field of light that
surrounds them." James explained.

"I do too," Ann replied, "so I guess we are both not
hallucinating unless our perception is being affected by our
extreme state of love."

James responded, "No, I think our perception of things
is being heightened and that is why we are seeing halos
around everything. But that brings up another question or
problem!"

"What problem could we possibly have?" Ann
exclaimed, "Other than my parents are going to be very angry
with me for spending the night with you, James?"

"Oh right," James replied, "I was not even thinking of
that problem, is that selfish of me?"

"No James," Ann responded, "It could ruin our

mood, and the high we are experiencing is way more important to me than how my parents feel, but I did not intend to cause them worries."

"Me either," said James, "but the problem I was talking about is: what is really love and what love really is?"

"Wow," Ann exclaimed, "are you trying to make my head explode with trying to decipher the answer for those questions?"

"No Baby," James laughed, "everyone uses the word love but it seems to me that nary a one of them knows what it means. Mary Baker Eddy says 'God is Love' and also says 'God is Spirit.' So could we say that if you distill these things to their essence, that Love is Spirit?"

"James," Ann yelled, "that is brilliant! How did you ever arrive at that conclusion, because I never saw that explanation in Mrs. Eddy's *Science and Health*…. did you?"

"No, I do not remember such, but it just came to me," James said.

And then Ann chimed in, "And that means that love is energy because you and I have already decided that Spirit is energy, right?"

"Oh Baby, you are so, so right!" James replied. "You are so correct! You are so schweet!"

"Wow," Ann said, "we are so smart! Well, I guess I should say that God is so smart and that in our state of sexual energy and relaxation, we can easily access Divine Mind, Divine Intelligence."

"Yes," James agreed, "we made another breakthrough into the hidden codes. Now, will anyone accept or understand what we have learned.

"Don't ask me," Ann said, "so far only that couple at the restaurant has listened us. I was astonished at that." James just nodded in agreement and they resumed basking in the afterglow energy, which just kept going on like nothing they could have ever conceived or imagined! Their bodies vibrated with the sensations of energy that coursed throughout their bodies like an electrical circuit.

Somehow, this electricity caused intense and extended feelings of ecstasy and euphoria. It would be many years until James learned just what caused this phenomenon, which would be well explained in Tantric and Taoist teachings! Regardless, he and Ann were in a trancelike state of wonderment and contentment! As they experienced the effects and results of the hidden codes they were most grateful for this!

CHAPTER 15

Soon after the prom, it was graduation night for James and Ann, and this would be the end of their high schools days. The more time that they spent together and the more intimate times they had with each other, the more they were tuned in to each other. They were starting to know each other's thoughts and they could often finish each other's sentences. It was like they had been together for many years, even though this was not the case. On this night, James did not even want to attend the graduation ceremony because he could not sit with Ann since people were seated alphabetically, according to their last names. Ann was still excited about the ceremony about which James was somewhat disdainful.

What James was looking forward to was the graduation party at Disneyland after the graduation ceremony was completed. And since everyone had just received their diplomas, the party was on! He boarded the bus with Ann that was headed to the Disneyland party. So on the trip to Disneyland, Marylyn and George, a couple and friends of James and Ann, asked, "What are you guys on anyways, some kind of trippy drugs? You guys are so amorous and affectionate, you must be having sex all of the time!"

And Ann exclaimed, "No, we are drugless and without alcoholic influences! And yes we dig each other so much that I guess it shows rather obviously, eh? And no, we don't have sex all the time, but we are always affectionate and we have found several miraculous things that result from our amorous adventures."

"What are you talking about?" George asked.

"Well," James replied, "We found when we become deeply affectionate, an extreme state of relaxation is created. From that state of relaxation, we are able to feel the energies of God penetrating our bodies and spirit, and the more this energy is created, the better and better we feel."

Marylyn then asked, "How did you guys ever figure this out? Because we understand what you are talking about!"

Ann replied, "We just kind of figured it out from our study of Christian Science, but realized that Mary Baker Eddy, the founder of Christian Science, never really talked about romance and even suggested that such things should be minimized because they were sensual and materialistic. But once you get around the Calvinistic influences under which Mrs. Eddy was raised, you can take her concepts and can expand them to understand things, especially romance!"

"How cool," George responded. "You two are becoming quite the philosophers, aren't you?"

James then replied, "Well I don't know if we are philosophers, but I know Ann would agree with me that we were tired of being ignorant about these things, so we took bits and pieces of ideas from here and there and we put things together. Even after the prom dance, when we went to dinner and a couple came up to us and asked us why we seemed so much in love. They especially noticed that we seemed to be glowing—or at least that is what they said! And when we told them what we actually discovered and comprehended, they a thought it was really insightful and they said we taught them things that they, themselves, as adults, did not know! How cool is that?"

George then exclaimed, "That is about as cool as getting tubed on a wave, right?" And James just smiled and nodded in agreement. "Hey James," George responded, "Do you want to go surfing after the graduation party?"

James then replied, "Normally I would but I would rather be surfing in a sea of love with Ann, after the party!" Ann just looked at James and smiled with a twinkle in her eye, as she knew that they would be creating some special magic between themselves. And she got excited just considering the possibilities. James then said "You know, George, when you are in the tube it feels real special and like you are kind of going into another dimension for a short period of time. Well, when Ann and I get that loving feeling, we are in another dimension for hours and I am not exaggerating!"

"I second what James said!" Ann replied. "We are so fortunate to have become a couple and learn so much and even experience what we have learned."

Oh God," James exclaimed, "it is beyond anything either of us could have and would have ever imagined was possible!"

"We have kind of cemented things together, right James?" Ann queried.

"Yeah, Baby," James replied, "we are together like 6000 PSI concrete and that is real damn strong!"

CHAPTER 16

The graduation party was a lot of fun for James and Ann… and George and Marylyn. But truth be told, they were all anxious to couple with their love interests after the party, since George and Marylyn were anxious to try the approach to love making that James and Ann talked about. Even James and Ann were giddy with anticipation since every time they became romantic with each other, even more incredible waves of energy would be created. The more they relaxed they were, the more energy was created between them and the more energy they created, the more relaxed they became and the stronger the bond and affection became between them!

So both couples got their motel rooms, each ready to experience tremendous bliss. One thing that James and Ann learned was the more trust they had with each other, the more they could relax. They also learned when they were somewhat tired, as they were from partying all night, the easier it became to relax and trust each other. All defense systems, such as the subconscious mind, which Mary Baker Eddy called mortal mind, were shut down and circumvented all hindrances to intimacy.

Also, the more relaxed they were, the more sensitive and tender to each other they became and again, the more electromagnetic energy was created and passed between them.

This was felt not only strongly in their hearts, but also throughout their entire bodies. When they got to their room, they undressed each other and James suggested to Ann they both put both of their hands in the air and put their hands close to each other without touching. Massive amounts of electricity literally passed across their hands and Ann's long hair began to kind of stand up. Even James' shorter hair reacted in the same manner. Ann felt waves of ecstasy shooting up and down her body, as did James. Ann exclaimed, "I don't know where you got this kinky idea James, but it eerily delightful."

"I don't know Baby," James replied, "somewhere out of the blue, but I do know I cannot keep my hands off of you any longer. I have to envelope you with my embrace and kiss you madly!" So he did just that, as did Ann likewise and followed his lead as he laid them both down on the bed.

Then they connected for an extended period of time with just their lips. What happened shortly after this was totally unexpected. Ann began experiencing short bursts of orgasm, which travelled far beyond her clitoris, enveloping her entire body. James experienced something similar and even ejaculated from his incredibly throbbing penis as he experienced wave after wave of energy coursing throughout his body; he felt like his head might explode, as had his penis! James and Ann were both moaning with delight. James apologized for prematurely ejaculating, but Ann exclaimed, "Actually your timing was perfect since we were able to simultaneously share our orgasms. Your timing was perfect, Sweet Baby, James!"

"Actually, you are right. We can conventionally connect later in the evening," James responded.

"Right now, let's bask in what we have created." Ann then exclaimed, "Sweet Baby James, you did not even have to stimulate my breasts to get me incredibly hot and extremely high. What gives?"

"I guess we are proving that although the erogenous zones are important for catalyzing sexual energy, which is only just energy, it is the actual "field of energy" created that kicks things up and creates this blissful feeling!" James explained.

"Damn, you never cease to amaze me with your insights, James!"

"Well you continue to amaze me with your insights too, and your incredible sweetness and passion which you share with me," James replied.

So as they lay on the bed, in the sweet embrace of each other, James was incredibly partial to spooning with Ann, whereby he would lay behind her on his side with his left shoulder upward and he would nest Ann into his body from a prone position with her left shoulder pointed upward likewise. This exchange of energy was much more sublime and subtle than the sexual act itself. Ann exclaimed, "I now know why they call it afterglow, because I feel like I am glowing like a light!"

"Baby," James laughed, "you are a light and my shining star. The amount of energy I see around your body is astonishing. I have never heard of anyone talking about this surrounding field of light." Ann agreed as she smiled and nodded her head in agreement. After about two hours, they connected sexually again, in the conventional fashion and then again another three hours after that. James' testicles ached a lot, but he could care less because what he and Ann were experiencing just kept getting better and more intense!

Meanwhile, Marilyn and George were experiencing their own waves of euphoric bliss from doing just as James and Ann had explained was their discovered approach to sexual coupling.

When the couples met at the agreed upon rendezvous for dinner, James and Ann showed up a little before their friends. When George and Marylyn showed up, James cracked, "Oh, I know what happened, you guys got so intoxicated by the energy of love that you did not want to come here, right? That's quite ok because we had the same experience, ourselves!" Marylyn and George just smiled with glee and started laughing out loud as they conveyed their agreement with what James had just described.

"Wow," Ann replied, "you two look like Cheshire Cats that are real fat and lazy and contented. We are so stoked for you!"

"Thank you," they both replied, "Nobody could have better or more informed or incredibly wise friends. We were going about this sex thing all wrong, concentrating on fun with friction and that is not what the essence of sexual coupling is about," George exclaimed.

James and Ann looked at each other smiling in agreement. "How schweet all of this is," they both blurted out loud!

CHAPTER 17

James spent a lot of time surfing in the summer and Ann accompanied him to the beach. He found that when the waves were good, surfing was euphoric during the rides on the waves, because you are transformed into another dimension. But when the waves are bad, when they are not lining up and peeling off, then the feeling of euphoria does not manifest. With small, good waves, things still felt very special; with large, closeout waves, not only was surfing not as fun, but the heightened feelings were not there.

But when James was with Ann, things were always good. They did not argue or disagree about things because they had cemented a bond between them that few people of planet Earth have ever been privileged to experience! And it was because of the romantic energy they shared with each other; they found it problematic to even argue. Each time they conjoined romantically, they would go to a higher level of experiencing this special energy, even though one would think that they had gone as far as possible in generating it.

Really there was almost nobody they could relate to except Marylyn and George. When the summer was over, however, both James and Ann would be going to different colleges in different states, and James was concerned about the distance that would be between them, even though Ann was not. James could only see bad things coming out of the separation and he did not want to be separated from or to lose Ann to someone else. "Don't worry, Sweet James,"

Ann said, "you know we were meant for each other and that is the way it will always be, right?"

"Yes I guess so," James said, "but somehow I have this weird feeling that we will be separated. I don't know how, but I just have this strong feeling."

Anyway, they went their separate ways at the end of summer. Ann was heading to Arizona State University and James to a local junior college. They did spend time together on some weekends and things between them remained unbelievable, as usual, as if unbelievable was usual. On the Thursday before they were to have a weekend reunion, James found out that Ann had been involved in a fatal car accident. Hearing this news numbed James; stunned and so disoriented he really had no desire to live anymore. James frequently considered suicide because he felt like half a person without Ann—maybe even less than half. James took no great pleasure his intuition had proven true about the separation between himself and Ann, and he was so depressed it was like he was sedated with tranquilizers.

One night Ann came to James in a dream; she told him he needed to stay on Earth and spread the message of what they had created romantically. Later, James remembered responding to her in the dream… that she was his one and only soul mate and there was no one else that could replace her and that was that. Ann came to him in subsequent dreams, giving James the same message. Eventually, he realized that he should not kill himself, although he was sure that he would be lonely for the rest of this life. Ann came to him in another dream and told James he would eventually meet someone at least as good as her. She also told him she believed we all have more than one soul mate, actually hundreds of them. James thought to himself, *the bar has already been set so high. I cannot even imagine anything remotely like this happening.* "Well," Ann told James, "If your primary relationship is with God, you will never be lonely and you will be provided with an appropriate mate to be by your side. Please trust me on this; you can see it so clearly in the dimension within which I now exist."

Just as Ann had said, James eventually found another girlfriend during college that he really liked, even though she smoked cigarettes and he did not… and even though she was not as pretty as Ann. What James liked about this girlfriend, Lesley, was that she was extremely sensual and a fantastic kisser, among other things. She did not want to have conventional sex, but they enjoyed having oral sex with each other. And James became very taken with her presence! He tried to never compare her to the incredible Ann and accepted her for her differences. James just did not reach the levels he did with Ann because Lesley was not interested in the information in the hidden codes, even though her grandmother was a Christian Scientist. But James was grateful to have a feminine presence in his life; just being with her made him feel very good!

However, when James found out that she went out on a date with her ex-boyfriend, who was in the Army, James realized that she did not have the same dedication to him that he had to her. He ended the relationship—cold turkey—without ever confronting Lesley about the infidelity. James saw her the next week at a college dance where he first met her, said hello to her and her friend, and zeroed his sights on another girl, and danced the whole evening with her. He dated this new woman one time, but she was not open sexually, as James was used to with his women… so that was the end of that. He next met another woman at a Christian Science youth group and she was very aggressive, sexually, but that kind of scared James; he was afraid that he would wind up getting her pregnant because she did not like using contraception nor did she want James to do so either. So after three dates, James made a quick exit from this relationship.

James had still another girlfriend who he liked quite a bit. He had gone out on a blind date with her, and felt she had a nice face and a great personality. But when she smiled, which was often, she became extremely beautiful and light would literally emanate from her entire face. They had a couple months together and went to the beach a lot and enjoyed going to clubs to dance. They would become very passionate, but Janice did not want to have sex. James was all right with this since she was so enjoyable to be around and she loved to have fun and say goofy things. But Janice was from another state and had to go back to college at the end of summer and because of the geographical separation, the relationship became disconnected and ended because James did not want to correspond with Janice through the mail. She kept writing him letters and trying to get him to respond, but to no avail!

CHAPTER 18

James found it hard to believe he walked away from a woman who he liked and who was sexually primed to express herself. It was just the idea that he did not want to become a father. Several weeks later, at the same Christian Science youth group, he met Ann. Yes, another Ann, and he felt the angelic presence of the new Ann as he did with his first Ann. Ann Sands, the new Ann, also had a huge aura around her and she seemed to sparkle like the old Ann. She had many attributes that could be accredited to an angel! Her teeth were very crooked, but James was totally enthralled with her. Having just graduated from college, James was sure that this woman would be his wife. He truly could not believe how he found this new Ann, and at night he thanked his first Ann for her counsel through his dreams. Ann Sands was a beautiful blonde, but it was her angelic presence that really stunned and attracted James. He started thinking: *maybe this is the hidden codes in action, since it says in "Science and Health…" that there is unlimited good and unlimited supply in the universe.* This realization was exciting for James. Later in life, James would learn how this was true even from a scientific perspective.

Best of all, Ann was a Christian Scientist and had considerable knowledge about the "Hidden Codes of God." She really was into James also, even though he was somewhat immature for his age, being prone to doing the goofy things that his first Ann enjoyed immensely.

When he danced with Ann Sands, he was transported to ecstatic states like he was with the first Ann. *Finally,*

James thought, *I have met someone who is synchronized with me and my knowledge and surely great things will come from this."* And in fact, great things were occurring as per his first Ann. "Wow," James said out loud, "I would think this was too good to be true, but I am experiencing it and I definitely do not want to screw things up." So he moved very slowly, sexually with Ann.

Their kissing and petting transported both of them into great fields of energy and ecstasy. James was so taken with Ann that in a very short time he asked her to marry him. To James' astonishment, she turned him down, saying that she definitely wanted to continue to date him. James was crying inside; filled with disappointment, he definitely did not want to end things with his special Ann. So they continued to date and one night Ann said, "I really want to have sex with you but I must be honest in telling you that I had sex a long time ago with a teenage boyfriend."

James sheepishly admitted, "I had sex for a long time with my first true girlfriend and so I am being honest with you. What you did in the past does not matter to me and I hope it is the same for you." Ann nodded her head in agreement and James was both grateful for the honesty and relieved. "With my first girlfriend," James exclaimed, we went to incredible levels of energy and euphoria that we attracted through our romance. You and I have magically created the same thing and even more, so I know I am blessed beyond belief."

So Ann took James to a couch in a house she was house sitting, and she was clad in a scanty, silk-laced robe and laced panties, which were driving him wild with delight and anticipation. Ann descended to the couch; she opened her robe and James lowered himself on top of her. They began kissing passionately, with liberal use of their tongues; grinding and flitting about each other's mouths. James began to bite Ann's breasts and to kiss them passionately. Then, biting and kissing Ann's neck, James quickly slid down to her vagina and began to use his tongue to probe about and stimulate her. Finally, Ann was so aroused that she told James, "Please enter me with your penis. I want to feel you inside of me."

"I want to feel myself being inside of you, too," James said, as he entered Ann's vagina with his penis—just as she requested.

The amount of energy that James and Ann created between themselves grew exponentially, so much so that James had to concentrate intently on preventing himself from ejaculating. He was successful in doing so for a long time, as he contracted his anal sphincter muscles; Ann finally climaxed with a mind shattering orgasm and loud moans. Following Ann's release, James withdrew from her and put his penis on her stomach and humped it until he ejaculated and screamed in delight as waves of energy shot up and down his whole body, which quivered in delight.

"Good God," James exclaimed, "We are animals!"

And Ann replied, "Well if we are animals, we are divine animals and that staggering amount of energy we created and shared with each other is more than just animalistic, don't you agree James?" A slow smile crossed James' face; smiling in a way that Ann knew he agreed with her.

After a few quiet moments in which the two basked in the presence of the other, Ann said, "You know when you asked me to marry you and I said no?"

"Please don't bring that up, as it is too painful for me to consider and remember! I love so much and I dig you beyond anything you might be able to understand," James replied.

"Oh, Sweet James," Ann cooed, "I also love you very much and I do want to marry you. During our sexual encounter, I saw a different side of you that so blows me away. Your tenderness and caring for me really blows my mind. I know we will be very happy just loving each other so intensely that we will always be creating magic between us."

"That is the way I have seen things since the first time I set my eyes upon you," James exclaimed. "There was no question I wanted to be with you for the rest of my life and now it is happening and you have made me so very happy. I think I need to show you though."

"Well," Ann replied, "It took me a little longer to make my decision than you but I knew you were special from the beginning... even underneath all your goofiness."

"So, are you saying I am goofilicious, Ann?" James said.

"Yeah", Ann giggled, "and sexylicious also!"

"Well then," James exclaimed, "it is time for me to show you, once again, just how much I dig you, so relax and let the second act of this show begin! But before we do that, let us bask in this orgasmic energy that we just created."

"Wow," Ann exclaimed, "I have never even heard of this; maybe no one else even knows how to intensely create it, but I cannot argue with your assessment because I am literally experiencing it. That is really so very fortunate for me, right?"

James just looked at Ann passion filling his eyes as he stroked her soft face and long, flowing hair, and finally nodded in agreement. "Every time, we must strive to create this and surpass it, if possible and then we will be bullet proof from any and all assaults on our relationship, both from within and without." James exclaimed.

Ann was quick in her response. "Let's spend more time doing it than talking about it."

"Yes, let's, Baby." James responded as he cuddled Ann in the deep crevice of his arms.

CHAPTER 19

James and Ann got married about six months after they agreed to marry each other. They also agreed neither wanted children, although Ann was very worried that James would want them. James told Ann, "It is just way too difficult growing up on this planet, simply because very few parents and teachers and governmental authorities know anything about the hidden codes. So you spend all of your life trapped in mediocrity, the illusion of pain, and experiencing way too much disdain. Ann, both you and I were lucky to begin to transcend these things in our middle teen years, but how many other people can you list that even remotely perceive this other than Christian Scientists?"

Pondering James' comment, Ann's response was slow to come. "Everything you said is true but I was just thinking from the perspective of my health that I do not want kids." In the end, they agreed on the subject of children, which then allowed them to more deeply study Christian Science and other metaphysical disciplines. Their reward was a much richer and fuller understanding of "The Hidden Codes of God." Aside from their studies, Ann worked as an accountant and James started his own landscaping business. It was hard for Ann to apply metaphysical knowledge to accounting but it was immeasurably easier for James to apply it to landscaping designs and installations.

Before James would design or install a landscaping job, he would always visualize what he wanted to design or create and then manifest it into creation. Considerable time was spent at night designing jobs and then visualizing what needed to be done the next day to bring the installation to fruition. Because of this technique of visualization, James became highly successful in designing landscape creations, installing the planting and hardscape in a short period of time, winning awards for his highly innovative work, and attracting considerable wealth into his and Ann's life.

It was primarily the innovative and artistic expressions that intrigued James the most. Whatever was involved with what a client needed to have manifested, James was able to do it. He attributed this to what he learned from Christian Science where it was accepted as fact that all intelligence and wisdom flows forth from God. Mrs. Eddy said many times that God is omniscient, which means having all knowledge. God yielded the results that James craved and created; it worked well for James to realize this and have a humble approach of believing everything was of God. Having Ann do his accounting work also lifted a heavy responsibility from James.

Ultimately, what James and Ann learned in regard to the hidden codes was that as they focused the perception that their intelligence and creativity did not come from a brain, and that by following what Mrs. Eddy said about all intelligence coming from God, made them more efficient and creative and insightful, rather than depending on their own so-called intelligence.

The couple also remained aware that the majority of perceptions reflected pretty much that nobody other than Christian Scientists could accept the concept of Divine intelligence. Some people who had been on acid trips claimed to have insights into this, which led James to wonder whether he could trust their perception. It would be many years later before James saw the validity and correlation between these things including DMT, Ayashuca, Psilocybin mushroom and Peyote trips!

Unfortunately, as almost always happens in a marriage, as they immersed themselves into their careers, especially in regard to James and his focusing on professional success, there were fewer romantic couplings between them. James was going to law school at night and the studying it entailed was eating most all of James' spare time. Still, the energy the couple shared during these times was incredibly euphoric, satisfying beyond words and took their consciousness to higher levels of understanding. Both James and Ann had their perspectives and understanding of things continually stretched; myriad things previously unknown to them over time became understandable. They started to actually understand how all creation was more spirit energy based than material or matter based, but there were still things that they desired to understand more.

Ann started studying about reincarnation and astrology. James was somewhat unsettled by this because he did not see how it fit in with Christian Science and The Hidden Codes. Ann persisted in her new studies, however, even with James' disapproval because she felt blocked in her own search for spiritual knowledge, understanding of God, consciousness, and self-realization. Ann's understanding was increasing, but James found himself standing still, at least in his spiritual pursuits. This trend would continue until James suffered a collision riding his dirt motorcycle.

The accident occurred when James was riding up a steep hill, which had to be approached with a lot of speed in order to ride over a steep rock face near the top of the hill. James cleared the steep face of the hill, but was T-boned by another rider, riding perpendicular to James on a road at the top of the hill. Neither rider saw each other until it was too late to avoid the collision. Grating sounds of metal against metal as the other rider hit the side of James' motorcycle, throwing James to the ground and jamming his handlebar into his throat. James was severely injured, but the other rider, traveling forty or fifty miles an hour was not seriously hurt as he was thrown over the bars.

Time seemed to stand still, and finally James tried to stand up. The motorcycle had come to a rest on top of him and the other rider removed it from James' body. Pain ripped through James' entire body, except his head, which was protected by his motorcycle helmet. James' walk back to his truck was one of considerable pain; his motorcycle damaged beyond being able to be ridden. Uninjured, and not in pain, the other rider helped James load his motorcycle onto the truck after driving it to the scene of the accident. James was in so much pain nothing could suppress the moans rushing from his throat during the walk back to his truck and during the drive home from the motorcycle park, where he had been riding.

When James got home in his truck with his mangled motorcycle, Ann could see that he was in great pain hearing him moan, the first thing she said was, "I know you don't want to go to a hospital, but you really need to."

James then responded, "While I am in intense pain and hurt all over my body except my head, I will heal myself. I know you think this is crazy, Ann, but I will pull this off." The night that followed James' accident was one of pain compounded by more pain, but as James began to control his fear about the fact he had been injured and might not ever recover from the accident, the pain began to subside enough so that he could go to sleep.

James went to work the next day with his employees, but it hurt to do anything, including walking slowly. He basically directed his employees, but really could not work himself. As the week progressed, each day James was able to do a little more work. During this time of healing and even right after the accident, James tried to visualize himself as created from Spirit in the image and likeness of God, as per Christian Science protocols. The better James felt, the less concerned he was about his situation; he no longer feared that he could not heal himself.

James remembered a previous time when he was riding his dirt bike in the mountains, and he hit his knee on the motorcycle handlebars; when he got home that night the knee began to swell and was throbbing with intense pain. He called a Christian Science practitioner to ask her for her help in healing his injury. She said she would do a Christian Science treatment. After several hours, James could feel no difference in the swelling or pain so he called the practitioner at 2 a.m. in the morning to express his concern that his condition was certainly not improving. The practitioner responded by telling James that it was only his fear that he would not be healed that prevented the healing from occurring. She also admonished James to trust in the healing powers of God and to let go of his fear. James realized that the practitioner was correct in what she said so then he began reciting the "Scientific Statement of Being," which says, "There is no life, truth, intelligence, or substance in matter. All is infinite Mind, and its manifestation for God is All in all." It goes on to say that, "Spirit is God and man is His image and likeness." The power of these statements made James realize that he was not a frail being, comprised of degenerating matter, but rather made from the Spirit of God. And once that realization was made, the pain and swelling almost instantly left his knee. For James, these healing experiences were demonstrations of The Hidden Codes in practice and beyond mere theory!

James applied this past experience to his present situation; as a result, he started to become immensely better and almost all pain left his body. But James was still perplexed as to why this accident happened. And he talked to Ann about it and told her he could not understand why he was involved in the motorcycle crash incident. She sympathized with his anguish about the accident and could see he was very perplexed about the whole situation regarding the "why" of the wreck. So Ann suggested that they go a psychic fair and have James get a psychic reading on Saturday, which would be the next day. For some reason James agreed to Ann's idea although he did not completely like the plan. His dislike, however, was overcome by his need to try to figure out why the accident occurred.

So the next day James and Ann went to the psychic fair and there was an older woman psychic reader who James sensed could give him some answers. He sat down at her table and asked her why the accident happened. Her name was Gloria and she responded, "You were being impatient weren't you? That is why you were involved in that crash! This happened on your motorcycle, right?"

James replied, "That is correct, I wanted to ride up this difficult hill and someone tried to ride up it before me and

86

did not make it to the top; it took them a long time to get off the hill. When they finally got off the trail on the hill, I was so frustrated that I proceeded to ride up that hill faster than I ever had before and I guess my speeding up the hill could have caused the accident." Then Gloria just nodded in agreement as did Ann.

Suddenly Gloria blurted out, "You were hurt very badly! Did you go to the hospital? You need to go to the hospital as you have been severely injured!" James then responded, "Yes I seemed to be severely injured but I did not go to the hospital nor will I because I can heal myself."

With an incredulous look, the psychic insisted, "You absolutely need to go to the hospital and be thoroughly checked out by a doctor!"

James was adamant. "I am almost completely healed and I will not go to the hospital, but thank you for your concern. I am a Christian Scientist and we do not go to hospitals, but rather rely on the power of God to heal us because in reality, we can never be sick or injured anyway!"

Gloria was astonished by James' responses and just shook her head in disapproval and said, "Remember that I told you that you were severely injured and you need to go the hospital to be examined."

"Thank you," James said, "but I am basically healed already other than my throat, and although I cannot talk very loud, my throat no longer hurts, so I feel so very blessed and healed by knowing the truth about myself, which no doctor ever knew or will ever know."

This accident was going to be the beginning of an intense quest by James and even Ann to learn more about

Robert J. Newton, J.D., N.D

The Hidden Codes and information of God beyond Christian Science and a fascinating journey it would be!

CHAPTER 20

T he fact that Gloria, the psychic, could tell James what had happened to him without any prompting, really impressed both James and Ann. They both were very motivated to learn more about psychic knowledge and other spiritual disciplines, other than Christian Science. James, in particular, was upset at the Christian Science mindset that you were not suppose to study spiritual disciplines other than the things contained in *Science and Health*…. and other related Christian Science material. Ann reminded James that they both had learned so much from the science of Christianity and had been so blessed in studying and applying its principles.

Ann further reminded James, "You will learn after some time that you never wasted your time in Christian Science."

James replied, "I never said anything about wasting my time, but I am pissed that there are things I should have known that I do not know."

"Well," Ann said, "I have a feeling that we will be learning a lot of new things very quickly! Why don't we take some classes at Psynetics, that place I was telling you about earlier and we will be on our way to a deeper understanding of 'The Hidden Codes of God'."

"Yes," James responded, "we really need to take those classes about Theosophy and Astrology and anything else!"

The couple enrolled in night classes at Psynetics and even before the first class they attended was over, James and

Ann knew that they had made the right decision. They were sponging up all the information to which they were being exposed. They learned about other spiritual levels and dimensions that existed, including the astral level wherein ghosts and spirits are inhabitants. Now, thirty years later, James was learning that in fact there are numerous ghosts and spirits that inhabit the entire Earth, with some places having more activity than others. Finally, James had the validation of all the spirits and entities he had sensed and felt in his bedroom when he was a small child. "How nice it would have been to have known this decades earlier," James mused.

James embraced the extreme sense of validation for what he knew many decades earlier when no one believed him or could explain it to him because it was part of "The Hidden Codes of God." James was thinking that these codes of God were deliberately hidden because almost no one knew about them or even talked about them. James and Ann would learn more about these hidden codes in short order!

At Psynetics they learned about reincarnation. James had never considered it as something really valid, apparently ignoring the information in *Science and Health with Key to the Scriptures,* where Mary Baker Eddy said that heaven could not be attained in one lifetime. Ann was more open to these concepts. So was James after he read, *Reincarnation: The Phoenix Fire Mystery*, by Head and Cranston.

In this book, James learned how reincarnation is present in almost all religions and many philosophies, but such information has been hidden, just as James had suspected, about the hidden codes he had been contemplating through much of his life.

James also learned how the overt references in the New Testament of the Bible were erased during the Council of Nicaea in Constantinople, Turkey, where the Catholic Church was headquartered before relocating to Rome, Italy. Apparently, King Constantine's wife convinced him to have reincarnation eliminated as a Biblical teaching, because she detested the idea. In the process of appeasing his wife, King Constantine had two newly coronated Popes killed because they would not accede to his wishes. The third newly installed Pope realized that his fate would be death if he did not renounce reincarnation so he dutifully complied and the rest is history.

Only the passage where Jesus said, "Before Abraham was, I AM," was left as evidence of reincarnation and this was not overt. So then James and Ann realized that the fact reincarnation had been expunged from the New Testament allowed the church to easily manipulate people with the fantasy idea of Hell. This was the idea James had rejected when he was five years old. James and Ann then thought about how the Christian doctrine of having to be forgiven for your sins and accepting Jesus Christ as your only savior, was patently unfair to Hindus, Buddhists, Moslems, and Jews. James said to Ann, "What kind of a cold hearted bastard would condemn more than half of the world's population to the fiery confines of Hell?"

"Like you said," Ann replied, "a cold hearted bastard. That certainly is not the God I know and feel. This whole concept is so incredibly unjust that it could not come from God! God help us if it does!"

"Don't worry about that," James replied, "Someone who took so much time and effort to create us and our surroundings certainly would not be so nihilistic as to condemn us with such a fate. It just goes to show you how far the hidden codes have been subverted and obscured. I truly feel sorry for people who center their whole life on this idea. At the very least, it shows that there has been no discernment in regard to this hell scenario and that blind belief is the modus operandi in this depiction."

"But that is what the Christian doctrine is based on," Ann replied, "blind belief. You must believe and accept the doctrine as absolute Biblical truth."

Then James responded, "Apparently they have not studied the 'Gospel of Thomas,' one of the texts that were excluded from the Bible. Therein, it specifically says, 'Belief without understanding is of little value.'"

"Are you kidding me," Ann yelled out, "it actually says that?"

"Yes," James replied, "This is in 'The Lost Testaments of the Bible.' It seems like that should have been the first book in the New Testament. So what we can clearly see is that there has been a concerted, orchestrated effort to deliberately hide the information of the hidden codes." Ann just shook her head with a resounding "No!" as an expression of disgust consumed her face!

CHAPTER 21

T he more James and Ann learned the "hidden code" knowledge was understood by very few people, the more they became obsessed about increasing their own level of special knowledge and understanding from new sources. In Theosophy, they learned of levels of reality never contemplated except by the most assiduous seekers of spiritual knowledge. They also learned of civilizations such as Lemuria (Mu), which was located in the area of the Hawaiian Islands. This ancient civilization existed over three hundred thousand years ago; they lived in peace and serenity and exhibited a high level of artistic and musical expression.

This civilization developed and utilized highly developed psychic abilities and practiced communication between the citizens via telepathy, which is the ability to send ideas and concepts and also receive them solely by thought energy impressions, in lieu of verbal communication. As James and Ann often knew what the other was thinking, they already had a well-developed level of telepathy between themselves.

James and Ann both conjectured about an entire civilization functioning on the principles of telepathy. Lies and deceptions would be worthless in such an environment. Virtue and honesty would be enshrined as the guiding principles to aspire to and display in a person's life. Contrast this with to the current governments and corporations on Earth, where honesty and truth have no premium value; where politicians tell the electorate things they think they want to hear, with no intention of really fulfilling the promises; where politicians take contributions from lobbyists and political interest groups in exchange for favorable legislation and favors: and where CEO's and other corporate officers routinely lie about the safety and effectiveness of their products, are involved in insider stock trading, and reap huge profits from secret (non-public) information!

Not to leave any stone unexamined, James and Ann learned about the civilization of Atlantis, a scientifically advanced culture whose technology vastly outpaced their emotional, social, spiritual, and knowledge base… to keep things from going astray or destroying an entire continent. The ancient Greek philosophers made references to Atlantis, including Plato, Sophocles, and Herodotus.

The Atlanteans had highly developed propulsion systems for spacecraft and air transportation. They had unlimited electrical energy generation and transmission without the use of fuels or electrical wires. There was travel to other planets, such as Mars, where there was a thriving and advanced civilization containing the best aspects of Lemuria and Atlantis. There was space travel to star systems that included Sirius, Pleiades and Andromeda. All of which had very spiritually advanced societies, aside from the technological wonders. However, somehow, someway, this did not translate into being spiritual upliftment for the vast majority of Atlanteans. As a result, their civilization literally crumbled through the misuse of Scaler wave technology; it created earthquakes of a severe magnitude and caused the continent split and sink into the ocean!

Then, James and Ann learned about astrological influences that literally shape the personality and outlook of an individual person. Both James and Ann found this knowledge very useful in understanding other people who have had things imprinted into their psyche by the placements of the planets and stars. They were given to understand astrological traits were tendencies and people did not have to be trapped in anger—a trait often associated with Scorpio and Capricorn. According to these beliefs a person could not use these less evolved traits as an excuse, or continue to expect embracing less than optimum and beneficial behavior. Unfortunately for James, he inherently reacted with anger whenever he was disappointed with something, or when events did not go his way and he wanted things to be quickly manifested.

The couple spent time to learn how numerological influences can also shape our personalities, similarly to astrological influences. But maybe the most beneficial thing they learned was how to meditate at the Crystal Cave Bookstore. Not only did the store carry many books on spiritual subjects, and hence were insightful in explaining "The Hidden Codes of God," they also carried crystals, had classes on meditation, and conducted group meditations. While this was not a problem for Ann, James severely doubted that he was even capable of sitting and meditating since he was a constant bundle of energy and never sat for any significant period of time other than to eat, or to watch TV or a movie. Then James' meditation teacher at the Crystal Cave, Robert Black, directed James to read Ram Dass's book, *Journey of Awakening: A Meditator's Guidebook*, and therein James learned meditation could in fact take place during even strenuous exercise and activities.

This revelation was insightful and liberating for James since he realized he could be meditating while surfing, skiing, riding his dirt motorcycle, and even while he was landscaping. James also realized, as Ram Dass' book revealed, meditating could be done in a sitting position more proficiently if done in union with diaphragmatic breathing done by breathing into the area just above the stomach, known as the diaphragm. This precise breathing regimen involves fully inhaling into the diaphragm through the nostrils and exhaling in equal fashion in the same manner, resulting in a deeper state of relaxation, also promoted by more oxygen infused into the body.

So from this, James felt liberated and as he became more proficient during his sitting meditations, his psychic abilities were enhanced and/or re-awakened from childhood. His experiences were just has Robert Black predicted and also reinforced by Ram Dass' meditation book. James and Ann were acquiring abilities of precognition, whereby you know things about events and people even before they happen. And as their intuitive abilities increased, they were able to get cross-verifying insights into the information about Lemuria and Atlantis from the Theosophy teachings. So now they were becoming code breakers and interpreters of "The Hidden Codes of God!"

Also, both James and Ann found that doing meditation in a group format made meditating easier and they reached much deeper levels of God infused energy, known as Prana, Chi, and life force. In other words, they felt more fully connected and directed by their Creator and their feelings validated this. Due to this higher level of God energy the couple experienced, they became quite addicted to the meditation groups and also found new friends with like-minded, understanding—people who were looking for a

higher life purpose and were striving to uncover such—
likewise basically searching for the Hidden Codes of God.

James and Ann' olds friends and families could not
understand the determined foray into their spiritual studies
but to James and Ann it just did not matter because they were
consumed with learning more of the hidden codes. The only
way to accomplish the goal was to pursue as many spiritual
disciplines as possible. Both had learned so much about the
coveted hidden codes through Christian Science, Theosophy,
Astrology, Numerology and meditation but their heightened
intuition indicated there was so much more to uncover and
absorb. And no one and no thing could or would stop them
in the relentless pursuit of knowledge and understanding
related to the hidden codes!

CHAPTER 22

Another discipline that James and Ann pursued was Tai Chi, a defensive Chinese martial art. Tai Chi is essentially a Chinese standing meditation technique which includes and choreographed series of movements and appropriately enough, a discipline called the "Standing Meditation." A Tai Chi grand master had taught their Tai Chi teacher, Tim, and while their teacher was younger than themselves, he had wisdom and patience beyond his young age. The fact that Tim was at least ten years younger than James and Ann did not bother them in light of the fact of the teacher's great proficiency and knowledge of Tai Chi.

The first thing that Tim had the participants do in the class at the Crystal Cave Bookstore was learn the Tai Chi "Standing Meditation." James was quite intrigued with this concept of standing with the shoulders sloped forward and the arms and hands hanging relaxed and the knees bent and then performing a diaphragmatic breathing with the mouth closed. While doing the exercise, the instructions were to bring a column of white or golden light from the heavens above and down the spine to an area just above the stomach and creating and accumulating a ball of light. And lastly, carrying part of this energy down through the legs and feet and see it anchored into the ground. All of this was done with closed eyes.

James and Ann had no idea of what was about to happen, but within a minute or two they began to feel a tingling and warmth in their hands and then around the area of their heads and spines. "Wow," James thought, "this is really so energizing and yet concurrently relaxing. I wonder why it is known or practiced by so few people. Ann did not necessarily like the idea of standing for a meditation, yet she could not deny that it was both energizing and relaxing. She actually was more enthralled with the Tai Chi form—the choreographing of very graceful movements, which she and James would subsequently learn. What happened after ten or fifteen minutes of the standing meditation was that everyone in the class began sweating profusely and their bodies were afire with energy!

On the other hand, James was captivated by another aspect of the standing meditation, called the attraction and repulsion of hands, whereby the hands were raised to about chest height without using muscle power. This is done by visualizing you are in a pool of water about chest high and allowing the hands to float upward with relaxed arms and hands. Then the hands are turned toward each other at about shoulder width and a positive charge visualized in one hand and a negative charge in the other hand. This allows the hands to pull closer to each other without muscle power and then when the hands almost touch, the charge is switched to positive in both hands or negative in both hands so that there is a repulsion of the hands without muscle power and the hands separate effortlessly. The process is repeated, and as this occurs, a ball of light is created and the hands become extremely energized. James was thinking that this would be a good pre protocol for energy healers who employed hands-on healing, whereby energy from the hands is directed to the body to create healing, using a hyper pranic energy or life force.

James and Ann next learned the Tai Chi Form or series of movements and Ann, having been a dancer, found the learning a wonderful one. Even James could not believe how much grace he acquired from learning and practicing the Tai Chi Form. He would translate the acquired graceful ability into surfing and skiing and working. What resulted from learning the form is that James learned not only how to be more graceful, but more relaxed when he did anything, even riding dirt motorcycles!

James and Ann shared their Tai Chi training and agreed how incredibly energizing and relaxing it was, but also how it increased a person's psychic and intuitive abilities. Ann also mentioned how it was already translating to the wonderful and tremendous sexual energy, when she coupled with James, into something even more intense. And James agreed and added, "I thought I might be hallucinating about this and I am so glad that you shared this with me, Ann. I am noticing and experiencing what you are. Although Tai Chi is well known in China, it remains a hidden code in the Western world. Just look how much we have learned in such a short period of time about hidden knowledge and practices."

Ann enthusiastically agreed with James and smiled profusely and summoned James. "Please take me in your arms and share your energy with me," Ann pleaded.

CHAPTER 23

James took Ann into his arms, and felt so blessed that he had Ann as his wife and also because they had both done Tai Chi, earlier in the morning. James and Ann could both see how the Tai Chi "Standing Meditation," was increasing their intuition and energizing them in their daily lives and inspiring them sexually, most likely because while they were more relaxed they were more infused with Chi, which is the essence of God. Both James and Ann learned from studying Taoism that there was a long tradition involved with this and Tai Chi; it was not just some new fangled trend or fashion. Steven Chiao detailed this in his writings and James and Ann could tell that it was based on a long line of experience and more like science than religion. It was detailed how as more Chi, or life force energy is infused into the body, health and spiritual enlightenment inevitably followed, as well as sexual energy and the prowess attached there from.

Ann was likewise delighted that she and James were led into more and more incredible emotions. As she began to tenderly kiss James, he responded in kind and the more they kissed, the more the energy between them was enhanced. Just the act of kissing Ann was comparable to both James and Ann's first sexual encounter involving penetration. Truly, it was like living in a perfect dream where everything was so right as energy circulated between their bodies and enveloped them incessantly so that things just kept getting more intense and the intensity lead to them feeling heighten desires. They thought they would reach a certain point where this sexual intensity would eventually level off, but it did not.

James then spooned himself into Ann's body while they were lying on their sides. James asked Ann to flip over on her other side so that her left shoulder was facing upward because he knew this would enhance their relaxing and have more sexual energy. As James was spooning into Ann, he caressed her breasts, which sent waves of ecstatic energy throughout Ann's body. She likewise shared this with James, so he was more than motivated and rewarded for his efforts. The energy was transferred to James with more intensity when he and Ann were connected with their hands. James also softly kissed Ann intermittently between caressing her breasts. As he and Ann lay on their sides, spooned and enmeshed with each other, amazingly, more waves of mind-boggling energy washed over them. Essentially as satisfying as actual sexual penetration with a finger, a tongue, or with the penis, neither he nor Ann was in a haste to advance to actual sexual penetration, because they were both having multiple orgasms and extremely intense ones at that!

The spooning lasted for several hours. Finally, Ann told James, "I want to feel you inside me baby. I want to be filled with you." So James obliged her command and pushed his head between Ann's legs and began to penetrate Ann's vagina with his tongue. He darted about her clitoris many times, although Ann was well lubricated and a strong vaginal odor was easily detectable to James. He liked this anyway, so it was just more of a turn on for him. And the more excited he became, although he concentrated on staying relaxed as possible, the more reactive and energized Ann became.

Because of this, there was a perpetuating experience that benefitted both James and Ann. Finally, Ann commanded

James, "Put your throbbing penis inside of me. I am about to explode!"

So once again James obliged Ann but directed her saying, "Get in the doggie position because I am about to explode, likewise, and I want to make sure that I do not climax before you. Ann indulged James and he entered her vagina from behind as he squeezed his anal sphincter muscles so that he could control his ejaculation. This being accomplished, he was able to concentrate on bringing Ann to a climax. However, rather than vigorously pushing back and forth inside her vagina, he was slow and deliberated his motions. But as Ann was coming close to orgasm he began to thrust into her with more force and just as she was nearing climax, James began to loosen his anal sphincter muscles so that he could unleash his orgasm in conjunction with Ann.

By this time they were both primed for a simultaneous orgasm, but before James would release his sperm, he made sure that Ann was at the beginning of her orgasm. And as she began to breathe heavily and was beginning to moan in delight, James then allowed himself to unleash the serpent power of his sperm. He yelled with delight as this occurred and screamed to Ann how much he loved her. They were both priming each other and feeding off each other's sexual energy. Their heart chakras were already open but the figurative doors to their hearts were blown off of the hinges! The couple became more and more enamored with each other, even within the experience of their conjunctive orgasms. Actually, Ann had successive waves of orgasms even after James was already finished with his climaxing. Not only was Ann in a state of indescribable bliss, but also so was James as he felt each multiple wave of Ann's orgasm.

After four orgasms, Ann was finally finished and she and James reclined on the bed in each other's arms. They caressed and smiled at each other, as they gave thanks for what they had experienced. After some time had passed, both James and Ann agreed that this sexual experience had led them to a deeper level of experiencing the presence of God, which is the essence of "The Hidden Codes of God." They attributed much of it to their practice of Tai Chi, and knew they had experienced more intensely the hidden codes... and grateful for it. The greater amazement was that they were getting more insights and answers to things they had been thinking about but could never completely understand. They did discover after this intense sexual encounter, heightened clarity about these things, including more insights into how sexuality could actually be an intense spiritual experience, regardless of what any religion or person said to the contrary.

James and Ann remained in each other's arms for almost an hour after their orgasms; they were in no hurry to do anything else! In such a state, their psychic abilities were activated very fully and it was nice to be able to understand things with such profound clarity! Things they had been thinking about, but could not resolve, became self evident with little or no effort at all. This included understanding the foundation of creation, which James was sensing was atoms, and the structures and forms in which they were manifested!

CHAPTER 24

The thing James and Ann were realizing was the more they learned about "The Hidden Codes of God," the more they were able to experience the actuality of the creator—to literally feel the evidence that God actually exists. Their meditation teacher, Robert Black, taught a couple of additional classes they took at the Crystal Cave Bookstore. He knew a lot of things about crystals and pyramids, as well as meditation.

In the crystal class, James and Ann learned about the characteristics of piezoelectric stones; they contained a static electric charge that always emanated an electrical charge. Robert explained that Tourmaline had the strongest charge, followed by Topaz and finally Quartz having the least energy. And yet when they put a Quartz crystal in their left hand, and lightly squeezed it, a detectable pulsing of electricity could be felt in the hand. It was concurrently energizing and yet relaxing. It was as though God was creating and contained within this piezoelectric charge.

The left hand for most people is the receiving hand, as was explained by Robert, and when James held a piece of Topaz in his left hand, he liked the energy more than Quartz; when he held a piece of Tourmaline in his left hand he liked it best of all. Ann felt that there was more than enough energy in a Quartz crystal. When the minerals where held in their left hand while they meditated, James and Ann were able to quickly relax and get into a meditative zone and elevated consciousness much easier than without the use of the piezoelectric minerals. According to what James and Ann learned in their class, a natural flow could be established whereby a person could transport himself or herself from Earth into another dimension. This was just another aspect of the hidden codes that confirmed what James and Ann were feeling: that these concepts were deliberately being withheld from the population at large. As a result, most people remained ignorant of things that could elevate their consciousness to be in a position the privileged elite, known as the cabal or Illuminati, could no longer control them.

James and Ann found that if they used a mineral such as Lapis Lazuli or Sugilite, it helped them see things from the past or what might occur in the future, even though they had no piezoelectric properties. James and Ann could feel the energy contained within these minerals, and learned that Lapis was often used in the crowns of kings, queens, and clergy, especially for the intuitive properties that were contained therein. The depth of this knowledge had been known for hundreds and probably thousands of years, yet known only within a very tight circle of elite and privileged people, including the hierarchy of the Catholic Church!

In the pyramid class James and Ann learned about the properties of the pyramid, which seemed to be the same or very similar to the energy of the piezoelectric minerals. They bought some pyramids from Pyradyne, a company founded by NASA astrophysicist, Dr. Fred Bell. Dr. Bell talked about how a pyramid was a cosmic antenna that focuses very concentrated energy that travels downward from the apex.

Again, the pyramid had the same effect of energizing the body and expanding consciousness and promoting a state of deep relaxation. This pyramid information James and Ann absorbed, and tremendous amounts of other information were contained in Dr. Bell's book, *The Death of Ignorance*.

The pyramids they were using had twelve-inch bases; they were holographic and not covered solid. Robert had James and Ann use the pyramids over their heads so they could activate the pineal and pituitary glands. These glands were believed to be associated with Chakras, which are major energy centers in the body as per Taoism and Yoga. They are associated with Chi, Prana, life force, or Universal energy. Almost as soon as they put the pyramids on their heads, James and Ann could feel a tingling on top of their heads as well as the area of the medulla oblongata—the soft spot in the back of the head—and the spinal column. One side of the pyramid base was basically had aligned with their foreheads. As with other piezoelectric minerals such as Quartz, these pyramids are known to facilitate vastly easier and deeper states of meditation.

James saw a book at the Crystal Cave Bookstore, *Pathways to God: Experiencing the Living God in Your Everyday Life*, which piqued his interest. He decided to buy the book and he was so glad he did, for there was information in this book he did not know even existed that certainly was related to the hidden codes. The book, written by Dr. Robert Newton, had volumes of information on the properties of various minerals and the states of consciousness and healing. James just could not believe what he learned from it.

In *Pathways to God....* there was information which revealed an eleven megahertz resonance between Quartz and pyramids. The book detailed how putting the base corner of the pyramid aligned with the forehead would create a more powerfully felt energy in the head. It also revealed that adding quartz or other piezoelectric minerals to the apex and sides of a pyramid would work dramatically stronger than when these things were used separately. Then James found that adding magnets to the pyramid would also enhance the effects of relaxation and energy.

When James and Ann tried the ideas in *Pathways to God,* they found they achieved the meditative state immediately and could go to a deeper level of consciousness and easily feel surrounded in a state of divinity. James and Ann were definitely grateful that they were so blessed to have attracted this information in their lives, because at a deeper level of meditation, problems and situations were all put in an optimum perspective; problems were solved and creative ideas flooded into their consciousness.

Additionally, James found information in *Pathways* that was from *The Rosey Tablets* by Gandalph Slick, which pointed out the part of the body affected by various pyramid angles. It also revealed that the pyramid angle fifty-two and a half degrees corresponded to the heart. Interestingly, that angle is exactly the same as The Great Pyramid in Giza, Egypt. This awareness would prove to be significant in James' life in the near future.

Regardless, James and Ann had learned many more aspects of "The Hidden Codes of God." And the information became purposeful in that the couple established more tools to work with by which their lives were enhanced! As more

110

understanding manifested in their lives, God became more than a remote concept but an actual working presence in their lives that they could sense and feel; this extended into Ann and James' sexual encounters, likewise!

CHAPTER 25

The Crystal Cave Bookstore remained a mine, rich in material to dig into and learn and acquire. At one point in time, Major Virgil "Postie" Armstrong, a special forces Army Ranger, and source of great knowledge and insight, presented a class at the store. James and Ann met Postie in 1983 and he explained how he was part of the security detail for the "Roswell Incident," wherein a UFO crashed near Roswell, New Mexico. In a class at the Crystal Cave, Postie explained the strange looking body that was recovered, being gray in color with a strange head and body. He also detailed the features of the high tech spacecraft that was virtually undamaged when the crash landing occurred. It should be noted that this information was released to James and Ann before the public had any knowledge of the incident, even though the event happened about three decades earlier.

Postie assured James and Ann this was not an incident involving a weather balloon, as had been touted by the United States government. The information made James lean toward a position that if the government could lie about this incident, it could and probably would not tell the truth about other occurrences, related to virtually anything. James was already extremely disillusioned about waste and corruption inside the USA government; he voted for Jimmy Carter in 1975 because of his pledge to downsize and consolidate 342 government agencies to be reduced to 16; yet none were ever instituted.

Anyway, aside from the issue of government credibility, Postie was well informed about many things that simply were unknown to other people. This led James, and even Ann, to consider that Postie might not have even originated on planet Earth. That he might in fact be of an intelligence, spiritual, and scientific understanding beyond that of humans. Any question they asked him about the spiritual dimensions, he could readily and unhesitatingly answer. During one class, Postie dropped a bomb on James and Ann when he proclaimed that there were at least eight dimensions basically coexisting in the same space.

This revelation had the effect of knocking James on his figurative ass, much more so than Ann. Postie was relating how the eighth dimension was the "unknown" and "infinity" and "oneness with the Creator." James did not have so much of a problem with the eighth dimension as he did with eight dimensions being stacked into the same space and place. In reality, it took James about three months before he could chew on this particular idea; it took about a year until he could swallow that, and another year to fully digest and feel comfortable with it. Many years after Postie related the concurrence of multiple dimensions, scientists would reveal "The String Theory" and "The Membrane Theory" explaining the very concept that Postie proposed; except they were talking about fourteen dimensions in the same space. So when James heard about these two additional theories, they were completely understandable to him.

At the time Postie revealed these things, James knew this was no ordinary person with whom he was associated. When what Postie revealed was stacked up against "String" and

114

"Membrane" theories, two decades later it became more significant.

So from these experiences with Postie, James and Ann knew that they had encountered a very evolved being who had significant knowledge of the hidden codes. Postie had very developed psychic abilities and he already knew what a person was thinking before they put it in words. One time he related something very significant to James when he explained, "There are people in these classes that say you are intimidating and they are afraid of you."

James responded, "I have been told that before. I think people are afraid of my knowledge and my power and yet they do not understand what they are afraid of, you know Postie?"

Postie then replied, "I know exactly what you are talking about as I experienced the same feedback earlier in my life. Well, anyway, James, I told them that they had nothing to worry about in regard to you because I told them you were in Jesus' inner circle and that I loved and trusted you!"

After a minute or two, James commented in a humble fashion, "I am most grateful for your confidence in me and your support of me. You know, us Scorpios are very often misunderstood. I have experienced this misperception many times; people either immediately really like me or they really dislike me, without even getting to know me. It is like I am being prejudged in both instances, whether it is favorable or unfavorable."

"So what you need to do," Postie explained, "is open your heart more because you have put a shield around it and some people, who are less aware and perceptive, cannot sense your innate and inherent divinity, as have I. You are truly incredible, James. You soak up new information like a sponge. It is a joy to have you in class, and Ann also, but she has already opened her heart and I wanted to share my insights with you, one extraterrestrial to another. You are suffering mis-programming in your sub consciousness from this and previous incarnations; it is mis-programming that prevents us from being our divine selves all of the time even though we can be nothing other than divine. And hence that is the game we have come here to play, to start out in ignorance and see if we can discover and share the perfection within us." James would remember this encounter with Postie as it would be the basis of the book, *A Map to Healing and Your Essential Divinity Through Theta Consciousness.*

So then James responded, "I know you are right Postie. During kissing and sexual conjoining, my heart is open off the chart. But the rest of the time I keep it hidden and protected."

Then Postie replied, "Let your light shine all of the time. Don't be afraid to keep your heart open. There are great things to come from you. Yes, I know you are already an incredible landscape designer and contractor but I am talking about really being a great teacher and leader of men and women. This is your destiny and your mission, like it is mine, and it could not be stopped anymore than a volcano ready to erupt and spew forth its magma."

"Oh! So you think I am a volcano, Postie?" James exclaimed as he laughed out loud uncontrollably.

"I did not mean that literally, James," Postie replied, "but maybe it is appropriate. Just be ready for this because it is in your future!" Postie's comments were going to prove much more accurate than James would realize at the time.

James felt compelled to ask Postie, "What about all that inner-circle-Jesus-stuff you were talking about? Did you really mean that?"

Postie replied, "How else would you have known at five years old that Jesus' teachings had been mispercepted and mangled. I remember you telling me this, but even before I told you that you knew Jesus like few other people on this planet, other than Mary Baker Eddy, who founded Christian Science and wrote *Science and Health*...

"Wow," James exclaimed, "I remember talking to you about Mrs. Eddy but I did not know you had a full understanding of her."

"Yes," Postie replied, "she was an extraterrestrial like you and I and Jesus. I cannot prove this with records yet, but eventually it will be known that Mary Baker Eddy was Mary Magdalene who was Jesus' wife and not a prostitute as related in Biblical accounts. Those were edited to our detriment, James."

"Cool," James exclaimed, "I always knew Mrs. Eddy was special beyond all words, even those she expressed in *Science and Health with Key to the Scriptures*. Did I ever tell you, Postie, how this book literally saved my life and most likely prevented me from committing suicide in exasperation because people could not understand the things I was telling them? And did I tell you how disillusioned I became with their lack of understanding and the stark and severe feeling of isolation that I harbored inside of me? I felt so misunderstood and lonely. Mary Baker Eddy's book literally saved my life here on Earth."

James then continued, "And then when my first girlfriend, Ann, came into my life, I became uncontrollably happy; she understood what I did and supported me as I supported her. What we shared could not be explained in words. Sexually, it was magic, and that magic bonded us at many other levels completely together and when she died it was like having my guts ripped out of me in a non-surgical fashion—without anesthetic. But you know, Postie, she came to me in my dreams from another dimension and she explained her love for me and that I should release myself from depression because shortly I would be meeting another incredible woman with angelic properties. And she was right; you can see quite a synchronicity here since her name is Ann, also, as you already know."

"Wow!" Postie replied. "I am borrowing your 'wow' phrase here because I think we have made some real breakthroughs; I feel a definite opening of your heart as we have been conversing here. That is so really special"

James responded, "I agree Postie, and Ann and I are most grateful for your sharing your wisdom and knowledge with us because you have revealed more of "The Hidden Codes of God," and brought them into a better understanding and perspective for us! We will be eternally grateful for having you in our lives!"

After a moment Postie exclaimed, "Don't ever forget your essential divinity! Those ingrained lines on your forehead indicate that you are a very old soul."

"I thought that phrenology had been debunked," James replied.

"There is a lot more validity to this than you might realize—something more than just silly superstition," Postie explained.

"Well, then," James replied, "I will keep my mind open on this subject. I am most grateful for your counsel!

CHAPTER 26

Still another avenue of learning from the Crystal Cave Bookstore came via the Tibetan Foundation. Somehow, Ann found out about this before James and wanted to make sure that James knew about this and would be attending this class with her. James asked Ann, "Just what is this about, this Tibetan Foundation?"

Ann replied, "It is based on the Theosophical writings of Alice Bailey, who revealed the information through her channel, Dwal Kuhl."

"That sounds way too cool to me, as it were," James replied. "We should definitely attend. Let's see what this channel can bring through. But I notice her name is Janet McClure, not Alice Bailey, who also channeled Dwal Kuhl. Why the discrepancy, Ann?"

Ann responded, "Janet is another channel of Dwal Kuhl and Alice Bailey has been deceased for awhile. James seemed somewhat occupied in thought, so Ann asked, "Did you get that, James?" James just nodded yes in response.

James and Ann showed up on Saturday morning at the Crystal Cave Bookstore. He was already impressed with Helena Petrovna Blavatsky (an occultist, spirit medium, and author who co-founded the Theosophical Society), who along with Charles W. Leadbedder (an influential member of the Theosophical Society) deciphered and diagramed the structure of an atom, decades before scientists discovered it.

When Janet began to channel, both James and Ann were amazed not only at the clarity of her message, but that she continually spewed forth information about reincarnation, the ascended masters of the White Brotherhood, and the various colored rays of energy coming into the Earth and how they effect people, places and things. This type of information fit into the category of hidden codes because again, it was not readily available or disseminated into the public through various media, including broadcast and publications. They went to several more events where Janet channeled Dwal Kuhl and the couple continued to learn more and had personal or general questions answered.

James and Ann even had private channeled readings from Dwal Kuhl through the conduit of Janet, which also pointed out their strengths and weaknesses. Then the Tibetan Foundation decided to give classes where people were taught to channel for themselves. These were called "Channel Clearing" courses and James and Ann attended one. Actually, James, with the coaching and encouragement of his meditation teacher at the Crystal Cave, Robert Black, had channeled a couple of times before. He even brought through information of the composition of the metal Electrum, which was used by the Egyptians and most likely, the Atlanteans.

Anyway, Channel Clearing used a series of meditations and toning (voice singing without words, relying only on sounds) to prepare people to be able to contact beings in other dimensions. James was unsure as to how well he was doing at this. But one thing he was sure of was that there was a rainbow aura over Janet's head and it was very intense and visible to James, although no one else in the class could see it. Several people received certifications of "Authorized Channel of the Tibetan Foundation." As Janet was awarding the certificates, she announced, "The last certification is going to a person who will be surprised by this award... the last award goes to James." And she was correct in her assessment because James did not perceive that he was worthy to be a certified channel of the Tibetan Foundation, but he was honored to receive such!

Ann received her channel certification at a subsequent Channel Clearing. While Ann shunned channeling in public, James took a liking to the idea because he felt it was a way to help people understand more things in their life. However, in the course of various public-channeling events, James noticed that sometimes the information from other dimensions came easier and seemed more accurate and useful than other times, when it was a real task to bring through the information. James had times of channeling where there was more than one channel and he found this more enjoyable since everything did not depend on him. One time in particular was especially enjoyable for James where he was the sole channel and brought some new and incredible concepts about the plant kingdom; including trees and especially roses, which James and the audience learned were the highest evolved plants of creation. James thought this was the zenith of his achievement in channeling and he received immense confirming feedback from the audience.

Actually, Ann, James, and several other people were involved in setting up a chapter of the Tibetan Foundation in California, which is how James got his many channeling opportunities. When James, Ann, and Dr. Spindle went to the board meetings for the national Tibetan Foundation organization, they started noticing a disturbing trend where channeling from the Planetary Logos, an overlord of Earth, was dispensing messages in contradiction to what had previously been channeled by Dwal Kuhl, an ascended master himself. After this Ann decided she had seen more than she could stomach or accept so she decided to distance herself from the Tibetan Foundation. James, however, despite his and Dr. Spindle's reservations, decided to stay devoted to the Tibetan Foundation. Spindle was especially outraged at how Janet seemed to manipulate the board of directors in ways that appeared marginal or outright unethical.

This was also the beginning of an impending breakup of James and Ann's relationship, although it was not clearly visible to either of them at that time. James continued public channeling and also began to give personal readings for others, related to their past lifetimes. He did not mind doing one reading for a person but when there were successive readings for the same person, James felt uncomfortable because some of the information he brought through was a repeat of previous things unveiled at an earlier reading. The one thing in these readings that James always avoided was asking leading questions because he felt that he should be able to get relevant information about a person's past lifetime without prompting.

Ann wanted James to leave the Tibetan Foundation and could not see why he could not see the inconsistencies and contradictions that were occurring on the national as well as the local level of the Tibetan Foundation. James felt Ann should be at his side and try to see things through or try to rehabilitate the Tibetan Foundation. Ann was tired of the dissention that was beginning to take a foothold in the group. James' problem was that he was grateful for receiving information about "The Hidden Codes of God," and could not bring himself to the realization that there was likely to be little more to be unveiled about the hidden codes in this group. In fact, James thought that the Tibetan Program protocol for clearing patterns and bad habits and less than stellar behavior from the subconscious mind was a brilliant revelation of more hidden codes.

Unfortunately for James and Ann this would lead to dissolving an eighteen-year-relationship, since James had found another woman in the Tibetan Foundation who agreed with him about the worth of remaining in the Tibetan Foundation. This woman, Michelle, was very attracted to James and he was likewise attracted to her! James loved Michelle's smile and presence and she exuded a sexuality and sensuality that was basically impossible to resist or ignore. As James and Ann were going through their divorce, his relationship with Michelle developed rapidly. James could not believe Ann would not support his position vis-à-vis the Tibetan Foundation and Ann could not believe that James was leaving her over this matter, especially in light of the way that they had melded together into such a cohesive unit. Additionally, Ann could not deal with the things that were churned up in her life because of subconscious clearing protocols of the Tibetan Foundation. In fact, Ann thought that these protocols were unnecessarily churning up problems between her and James.

Additionally, James and Ann were somewhat drifting apart and that could be attributed to all the involvements in their personal lives and the fact that they did not regularly show affection for each other, except during their now infrequent sexual couplings. And as James would figure out much later, this continual show of affection is most crucial to keeping a marriage cemented together. Although a lessening of affection is generally considered by society in general as something that is inevitable, James wondered why couples allow the pervasive pattern to manifest in their lives and diminish or ruin their marriages and relationships! He figured, people become numb to the obvious deterioration of their relationships and that familiarity with one's partner led to a state of boredom.

James could not see this at the time, but some years later he would realize that Ann had the more correct assessment about this situation regarding the Tibetan Foundation. Also, Ann saw many couples that were breaking up who were involved with the Tibetan Foundation and this synchronicity was revealing a recurring pattern that was more than just a random occurrence. People were telling James that his exit from his relationship with Ann was exceedingly hasty and misconceived. These people would turn out to be more correct than James' meditation teacher, Robert, who told him that his time with Ann should be over because they did not have much in common.

James was completely oblivious to all of this as he was under the spell of Michelle to a level where it was affecting his ability to make clear and unbiased assessments. Soon, James would be sexually involved with Michelle in a way like no other woman before, but this would come with an unperceived price tag and consequences. Again, these things would not be immediately apparent but would reveal themselves as time progressed

So as the inconsistent and unethical things occurred in the national Tibetan Foundation board meetings, they seemed to filter down to the California Tibetan Foundation chapter. James was asked by almost unanimous consent to run for the position of president. James declined the presidency but said he was open to the vice presidency. James did not want to become "drunk" with the power of the presidency and thought it would be circumvented if a woman held that position. That is precisely what transpired, just as James wished, but it would not be long until he was bitten in the butt by decisions that were made at a board meeting chaired by James because the president could not attend. The actions that were approved were undone unilaterally by the president, Marilyn, because she disagreed with the voted upon decisions by the board of directors.

James and two other board members vociferously protested the action, but Marilyn and the head channel, Terri Ferry, were determined to countermand the board's decision. James finally faced the reality that the California chapter of the Tibetan Foundations was mired in irreparable dysfunction. Lead channel, Terri Ferry, only compounded the problem; she worked behind the scenes to manipulate the California chapter through biased and unethical psychic readings she gave group members. A certain naiveté was being lifted from James' consciousness in that he had never seen women manipulate things in such an egregious manner before. The whole purpose of having a woman president had been completely circumvented. And the thing that shocked James the most was that neither Marilyn nor Terri considered any of their actions as wrong or detrimental to the greater good of the group.

The whole purpose of the Tibetan Foundation was to uplift humanity and bring them into a New or Golden Age and James was watching it all disintegrate. He voiced his concern to the national Tibetan Foundation that there was a need for them to intercede in the matter because there had been several violations of the California Corporate Code. James was told to remove blockages from his subconscious mind and everything would resolve itself.

James chose to ignore this advice; he found it pathetically laughable at best. He was glad for the things he learned in the Tibetan Foundation, including toning, which was a type of voice sounds like singing but without words, and concentrated on making overtones that could help eliminate blockages and sickness in the human body. James treasured and expressed gratitude to the professional singers who were involved in the Tibetan Foundation, for sharing their knowledge and teachings with him. Certainly, this was knowledge related to "The Hidden Codes of God," but James bid adieu to the Tibetan Foundation, the group that helped to destroy his relationship with Ann and begin a new relationship saga with Michelle.

CHAPTER 27

Michelle had a presence about her that exuded a tremendous amount of heart energy as well as sexuality. She also had other physical assets that were very appealing, including a nice figure, pleasant looks and an incredibly shaped derrière. The attraction between James and Michelle was mutually strong and it was as if sparks were flying when they were touching and kissing. Their first date involved a move that James used with his first girlfriend, the first Ann, where they went down to Newport Beach and danced on the shoreline under a full moon.

As far as James was concerned, this would cement their budding relationship into a bond that would make them inseparable and establish an unshakable foundation. The energy that was attracted into their mutual presence was overwhelming in its power. It caused a complete opening of both of their hearts, which was so exhilarating and euphoric that it would defy words. There was the pervasive feeling of prana/chi/life force/energy of God, which was intoxicating and enchanting beyond any hallucinogen or mind-altering substance. The joy shared during their embraces and dancing was more than either of their consciousness could completely understand or comprehend!

So compelling was the energy Michelle and James' attracted to themselves that it was spilling over to other couples walking on the beach and many of them began to follow the dancing lead of James and Michelle. Thus the energy resonance field that everyone shared was spilled over and transferred back and forth among all of the dancing couples. James was completely oblivious to all of this since he could see and feel nothing other than Michelle. Michelle shared her observations with James and asked him, "Do you see the other couples following our lead and beginning to dance with us?"

James replied, "No, and I could care less because I only have eyes for you. I don't see the other couples and while I am glad that they are enjoying their dancing with us, it matters very little to me, but you matter a whole damn lot to me! I sure hope you are feeling and experiencing the ecstasy that I am!"

"Are you crazy?" Michelle replied, "How could I not feel the tremendous energy we have created between ourselves? When you kiss me it is almost like an orgasm—in fact it is an orgasm of some sort and I will be rewarding you very soon."

"You already have", James replied, "because I am having a similar orgasmic effect myself! Damn, you are an amazing kissing machine. I can only imagine what you are like during a full sexual encounter. You might blow out my brains when we are fully conjoined!"

"That can and will be arranged," Michelle responded.

And in fact, that did occur as James and Michelle finally sauntered back to Michelle's car. They arrived at her car and sat down inside, where both beamed—happy beyond all comprehension and smiling profusely at each other. Then Michelle began to unzip James' shorts and began to massage his penis. Soon, she pulled down James' shorts and underwear and descended into his crotch and began to lick his penis. James was groaning in delight as her tongue felt like an incredibly arousing massage. Soon after Michelle's tongue work, James' penis had come to attention and was hard and ready for Michelle's next move, which was to put her mouth on his penis and suck on it very intensely. This created an infusion of prana, or life force, which James took in and circulated throughout his body.

James wanted Michelle to slow down and take a break so that he could orally please her. She ignored his recurring pleas since she was aroused by James' finger in her vagina. This was driving her crazy because he was probing her clitoris and even though she did not make much sound because his penis was lodged in her mouth, James could tell she was excited and likewise infused with prana.

James held out for quite a while before he erupted into an orgasm, knowing the longer he prolonged the pre-orgasm phase, the more intense it would be and the more flooded his entire body would be with divine energy. Likewise, Michelle knew this also and she could intuitively feel when he became more intense as she focused on her pursuit of James' penis.

James' moans turned into an ear shattering series of screams as he finally climaxed and it literally did feel if his brains were being blown out of his head due the tremendous amount of energy that was circulating throughout his head. But his whole body was like a tuning fork, vibrating with electricity that led him to ecstatic heights. And Michelle was also taking in this energy and she was also real damn high.

As James sensed the pitch of excitement, he seized on the opportunity to bring Michelle to her own "lift off" and pulled down her jeans and panties and plunged his tongue into her vagina. The odor of her pussy was like a catalyst that energized James even more. He rammed his tongue deeply into Michelle's vagina but then quickly receded with directing his tongue to her clitoris. And as he engaged, Michelle began to squirm and moan, but every time James sensed she was about to orgasm, he would remove his tongue and lick her inner thighs. It occurred six or seven times and finally, when James could tell that Michelle was higher than a satellite, he kept his tongue darting about her clitoris until she climaxed with powerful screams, making James' experience almost as happy and euphoric as Michelle's experience.

After James and Michelle had both climaxed, wrapped in each other's arms, they softly caressed each other and absorbed the energy they had created. For James, it seemed like each time he was sexually conjoined with a woman, the more it seemed to open his heart and add to his enlightenment. In fact, he realized an accruing light intensity occurred during his sexual encounters. James would have many other sexual moments with Michelle, and they would be wonderful and yet they never measured up to this first time they joined in sex. And eventually James would realize why, but it would be some time before this occurred!

In subsequent sexual experiences, she usually became guarded and somewhat combative after their sexual encounters. It was incomprehensible to James, because they created powerful waves of energy and euphoric states of consciousness. For Michelle, however, things in her sub consciousness interplayed into her interaction with James and she was not even aware of how and why this occurred. But for James the distraction was painful for him to endure.

CHAPTER 28

There were several parts of "The Hidden Codes of God," that factored into James' decision to go Egypt. However, getting there was an ordeal in and of itself since James was very engrossed in running his landscape design and installation business. James' meditation teacher, Robert, was constantly pushing James to make the journey to Egypt with the group of people he was taking there. In response, James would just tell Robert that it was just not possible to take off two entire weeks from his business. After a long and intense meditation, all of a sudden James knew he should visit Egypt. This decision was made despite the fact that Michelle could not get time off from her job as a schoolteacher to accompany James.

This was quite a surprise to James since he had a strong urging to visit Japan and learn everything about that country, but would never take two weeks off from work to visit it. He had never even previously considered Egypt. The trip there began with a flight from Los Angeles International Airport to Amsterdam for a layover. And in the short time he was in Amsterdam, James experienced a culture where the bicycle was as important as cars and where drugs and most things sexually related were considered legal, as opposed to the United States, which was obsessed with controlling drugs and sexuality. Actually, in regard to drugs, James already knew that the CIA, Mossad, and other intelligence agencies funded their black operations through the sales of drugs, and obviously they did not want to lose their sources of funding.

So with no legal sale of drugs, the prices received from the illegal sale of drugs would remain high and very profitable, thus eliciting more funds for the "off the book" government operations.

As for sexually related things, James figured they were regulated due to the influences of religions and a repressive and hypocritical mentality. James supposed that if there were more frequent sexual couplings, there would be more satiated human beings who would be less likely to entertain ideas of and participation in wars. James hypothesized that there is obviously not enough sexual activity in this world because there certainly is a continual stream of wars or civil wars occurring somewhere at sometime on planet Earth.

The next morning, after a beautiful evening in the lights and canals of Amsterdam that created a very romantic and enchanted feeling, the tour group departed by plane for a short stop in Turkey and then quickly proceeded to Cairo, Egypt. James experienced culture shock in Egypt immediately at the airport, where it was decided that his passport should be scrutinized. This was at a time in 1984 before airplane terrorists or terrorists in general were prominent. James could only think that he was being singled out because of his very bushy beard. The incident was delaying the departure of his group from the airport to their hotel in Giza, Egypt. After a considerable amount of consternation and examination of James' passport and the checking of the data related thereto, James was allowed entry into Egypt and the group proceeded to their hotel.

James' second culture shock event was related to just how crowded Cairo was with people and vehicles. Vehicle travel consisted of five lines of traffic on each side of the read, which was designed with three lanes accompanied by a lot of honking involved with the driving process. And yet there were no accidents involved with this driving scheme, nor were there "road raged" drivers.

Additionally, there was a haze of smoke and a less than pleasant odor in the air in Cairo. Aside from these things, James and the rest of the group were looking forward to the things they would be experiencing in the wondrous land of Egypt. For despite the conditions associated with Cairo, Giza, on the edge of Cairo, was very calm and tranquil and filled with pyramids, as well as the Sphinx.

After the group arrived at the Holiday Inn in Giza, they made a quick trip to the Great Pyramid before nighttime. Although they arrived too late to enter the Great Pyramid, they walked around it and the other two adjacent pyramids and some of the group, especially Robert, the tour leader, and James, could feel immense amounts of energy that radiated from these pyramids. There was a pulsing electrical current that could be detected if they were extremely relaxed. It was the relaxation that made the energy current noticeable and detectable.

As dusk arrived, the group headed back in taxis to the hotel and had dinner, amid the final Moslem prayer session of the day. The cool thing about this trip for James was that he had no expectations about what would happen in Egypt; because of this, he had no preconceived notions of what would occur there so there were no prejudicial filters to taint his experiences. But the discussions among the rest of the group that night was about what might happen in regard to spiritual experiences they might have, unlike James who was going to let everything come to him naturally. Yes, James knew of the power of pyramids from his use of the holographic type to meditate on top of his head but he had no idea what would happen inside a large pyramid form.

The next morning, at dawn, the first of the daily Moslem prayer chants was blaring throughout Giza and Cairo and it awakened James in a startled state. He went to the balcony and joined in a Tai Chi "Standing Meditation," which he and his second wife, Ann, had learned. After breakfast, the group went to the entrance of the Great Pyramid and paid a fee so that they could enter the King's Chamber wherein James and Robert would feel a pervasive electromagnetic field of energy. But there were other visitors and a guard in this chamber, so the group elected to skip the group meditation they had planned.

Next, they ventured into the Queen's Chamber and since it had no other visitors, the group held a hand linked meditation which was very powerful; much more powerful than if they had meditated individually. This increased group energy effect was compounded by the fact that many of the group were holding Quartz and Tourmaline crystals and were wearing various gemstone necklaces with Lapis Lazuli, Amethyst, Rose Quartz and Tourmaline. James was very appreciative to have the dynamic of the group energy so that he could get to deeper levels of meditation in the Theta level. And after this meditation, James realized that regular meditation at Alpha level was part of the hidden codes and at Theta was an even deeper aspect.

He only wondered why it him so long to make this realization because it had been staring him in the face for quite some time!

After lunch at a Giza café, James, Robert Black, and Robert Miller decided to take a walk to the top of the Great Pyramid, even though it was illegal to do so. With bribes to the pyramid guards and tourist police, anything was possible, no matter how illegal. So after paying the requisite gratuities, the three scaled the Great Pyramid with a guide. The ascent was much less difficult than James had anticipated and when they reached the apex of the pyramid, Robert Black and James began doing an extended Tai Chi "Standing Meditation," even though the guide kept telling them which direction Mecca was located because he wanted them facing in that direction, which was to the east. James and Robert Black could care less about the direction of Mecca, but acquiesced to the wishes of the guide to placate him. What they did care about was how much more powerful the "Standing Meditation" was for them on top of the pyramid—more powerful than they had experienced with Tai Chi in the past! There was so much electricity emanating from their hands and heads it was like they were electrical power generating plants. The group continued to do Tai Chi in its many variations and permutations for at least an hour. They could feel the guide looking at them in wonderment even though their eyes were closed. Robert Miller was photographing the whole sequence of events that manifested at the pyramid apex.

When they descended from the pyramid and went back to their hotel, the topic of discussion among the group, and many of the other guests of the hotel, was the crazy Americans and their strange moves at the top of the pyramid. James could understand this interest from one perspective, but not at the essential level. So he decided to share what he learned of Tai Chi with not only his own group but other hotel guests, telling them how it was not only calming, but energizing and that they could feel a distinct electricity in their hands, spine, and head. He also shared how he felt that at one time on Earth, at least most people in the Orient knew the things that were just re-emerging into consciousness, and that this was part of hidden codes or information shared with us by our extraterrestrial intelligence or Yoga Siddhas, Taoist masters, and others. As James and Robert Black explained and demonstrated Tai Chi close up and personal, they got the people in their group and some other hotel guests to actually participate with them in a session and once they experienced Tai Chi, the hotel guests could better appreciate what was involved!

After eating a late dinner at the hotel, James did another meditation session and went to sleep since the group would be having a special, private early morning special session in the King's Chamber. Everyone in the tour group turned in early in anticipation of the next day and its rewards. The group left the hotel so they could have as much time for their private pyramid session as they required. The session, of course, cost a pre-arranged fee, but everyone felt it was well worth the cost. As soon as they entered the King's Chamber of the Great Pyramid, the group was ready to meditate. The group replicated its hand joined meditation conducted in the Queen's Chamber and almost immediately all the women and men in the group could feel a powerful and deeper meditative state than which was previously experienced. There was a quantifiable difference that could be measured by the electrical tingling in their hands, spines, and heads. When this meditation was over, after about thirty minutes, the next phase of meditation commenced. It was a chance for each of the ten group members to get inside the sarcophagus, lay prostrate and begin an individual meditation. The sarcophagus was surrounded by the group members who channeled energy to the person lying down inside. Many in the group were holding quartz crystals in their hands and directing the energy from the points of the quartz into the sarcophagus.

When it was James' turn inside the sarcophagus, he entered with no special pre-conceived notions about what would happen other than a nice meditative experience. However, before even a minute transpired, James entered a state of extremely smiling bliss wherein his heart was completely opened. And then a tremendous surge of electromagnetic energy, identified in his metaphysical classes as life force, prana or chi, came blasting down into his head and filled his entire body in a fashion even beyond his most intense sexual experiences.

As his body resonated in a vibrating state, his consciousness completely left his body and he was viewing his body from above the sarcophagus and then he lifted into the vast reaches of space. James felt as though he was surrounded by the presence of God, and in fact, was sure he had been.

The entire experience was exhilarating beyond descriptive words and was chronicled with pictures by James' friend, Robert Miller. Essentially, James had a type of Kundalini experience, but with a softer progression of energy that was easier to adapt to and appreciate. Everyone else in the group had a nice meditative session but nothing like what James had experienced. He felt blessed for his intense melding with the Creator. But the experience was so intense that it would be a long time before James could completely understand what happened or how it occurred. One thing that became clear to James was the information contained on the pyramid angles in Gandalf Slick's *The Rosey Tablets,* was accurate. Slick claimed the pyramid angle of the Great Pyramid at 52.5 degrees corresponded to the heart and heart chakra. Because of James' heart opening experience therein, he knew that somehow—someway *The Rosey Tablets* contained more of the hidden codes.

Moreover, there was a small shaft in the great pyramid that once a year became aligned with the planet Sirius B for one day. Contemplating this, James thought that the pyramid surely could have been built by extraterrestrials from the planet Sirius B, possibly as a navigational aid. Really, what other reasons could be summoned for this most unlikely of coincidences and validate the deep research and writings of Robert Temple and possibly even Zecharia Sitchin and Eric Von Däniken? These three authors wrote about extraterrestrial cultures that came to Earth, many of them to mine gold. Temple's book concentrated on the Dogon tribe in Africa, where apparently a lot of gold was mined and the people there still have records of their ET visitors who came from Sirius B.

James intuited that since gold seemed to be in such demand in many parts of our Milky Way Galaxy, it must be related to The Hidden Codes of God. He knew that gold had an octahedron atomic structure and conducted electricity better than any other metal, and also knew Zecharia Sitchin wrote in his several books about the Anunnaki people from the planet Nibiru who came here also to mine as much gold as possible. For what reason no one seemed to know, but eventually James would gain insight into this.

After several days in Giza, including a visit to the Egyptian Museum in Cairo, the group left by plane to the city of Luxor, wherein two magnificent temple complexes existed. Including the fact that Luxor was situated next to the Nile River, it was an enchanting and beautiful place to be. There were numerous fascinating things that occurred in this new location. On their first day in Luxor, the group visited the Temple of Luxor, which was shown by Egyptologist, René Adolphe Schwaller de Lubicz, to be a symbolic replication of the human body, including the chakra energy centers contained within it. This, in and of itself, was amazing to James; that there was some kind of high intelligence that designed and built this temple. There were sacred geometries included, consisting of at least the Pythagorean formulas of Pi (3.141) and Phi (1.618) known as "The Golden Mean," and yet there were no records found of this knowledge being written into any codex or tablets in Egypt!

But beyond all these magnificent geometries and symbolic body representations, before he had walked one third of the distance inside of the temple, James flashed back into a previous lifetime. He wore the garb of a priest and saw two other members of the group, Robert Black and Robert Miller, dressed in similar garb of the ancient priests. Furthermore, James saw two rooms on the left backside of the temple that existed at one time and yet no longer appeared. All this happened as James was walking and awake with his eyes open—not even in the normal meditative state. At first James thought he must have certainly been hallucinating because he never heard of anyone having or relating a similar experience comparable to his. But Robert Black, who was an Egyptologist and had assiduously studied the Temple of Luxor, told James that the two rooms did in fact exist at one time and were diagrammed in Schwaller de Lubicz's research contained in *The Temple of Man.*

Wow, James thought, *what I have experienced and learned is just so amazing.* And yet James was about to learn more: that when you stretched out your arms with your palms facing outward, you could feel electromagnetic energy between the columns in the Temple. The feeling was both energizing and relaxing as per a Tai Chi "Standing Meditation." However, a negative aspect to it was having the guides in the temple snickering as James and the other group members experienced the energy between the temple columns with their outstretched arms. Once, again, in some way this related to "The Hidden Codes of God," regarding the static energy fields they contained! Was there energy that could be tapped into and distributed to power things from these granite columns?

In addition to the high mathematical and construction knowledge possessed by the ancient Egyptians, they possessed artistic and sculptural abilities probably never exceeded or equaled on Earth. This was evidenced, among other things, by the Avenue of the Sphinxes, which started at the Temple of Luxor and extended to the edge of town. There was a consistently replicated and highly detailed double row of cow sized Sphinx figures extending as far as the eye could see. Beyond this, there were ornate and symbolic pieces of artwork exhibited in the many tombs at the Valley of the Kings and the Valley of the Queens on the other side of the Nile River in the Luxor area. But James was more interested in the large obelisks near the Temple of Luxor, which generated an electrical field of energy similar to the pyramids. Could these structures have been used as electrical energy accumulators that somehow distributed electricity to the populace of Thebes, which is now known as Luxor?

Well, as awesome as the artwork painted inside the tombs of the Valley of the Kings and the Valley of the Queens, and the brilliant colors that had not faded for millennia and could not even be replicated today was, James was most intrigued by and anticipated the group's visit to the Carnak Temple complex. This complex really contained multiple temples built by different rulers and builders. The reason for James' inordinate interest was that the granite columns in the various temples had diameters of three and four feet and these would contain massive amounts of electromagnetic energy that he was intuiting answers to questions regarding his earlier thoughts about it.

Some of the people in the group, upon entering the Carnak complex, spent a lot of time experiencing the energy between the columns with their outstretched hands. Once again, the guides in the temple complex where having a snicker-fest, considering the crazy Americans had lost their minds. And in fact the crazy Americans had more accurately transcended their minds, perceived a higher consciousness and energy and did not worry about the misunderstanding of unperceptive simpletons! The fact that they could literally experience things about the hidden codes was too valuable for them to worry about the disapproving reactions of others.

Additionally, there were pictographs/hieroglyphs via paintings and stone etched reliefs that indicated how information and/or energy were transferred from one person to another. If the left hand of one person was opposed by the right hand of another person, then the left-handed person received information from the right-handed person. Robert

Black, the group leader, was very adept at understanding this and could read virtually any one set of hieroglyphs at the symbolic and higher level of depiction. This was in contradistinction to the Egyptian Egyptologists who read everything at literal and lower levels.

The group also took a trip to Saqqara, where there was the step pyramid of Zoser (Djoser) that was constructed of clay bricks. While the pyramid was not nearly as impressive and did not generate energy like the pyramids in Giza, it was the ruins of a temple complex that held the real wonders in Saqqara. This was because there was a row of cubicles where the seven notes of the diatonic scale could be heard if you put your head inside. The cubicles could have been used as a vibrational healing modality and thus it lead to more aspects of "The Hidden Codes of God."

In the columns of the Temple of Saqqara (Sakkara), members of the group were taking in huge amounts of energy from between the temple columns, including James. By now they were well versed and experienced in detecting the energy fields emanated by these granite columns. But for some reason, these columns seemed to have more energy than all of the others in The Temple of Luxor and the complex of Carnak Temples. And yes, the crazy Americans with their outstretched hands amused the guides, more so than in any of the other temple areas.

While there were many other things that occurred on the trip, the aforementioned experiences were the things James cherished the most. He could hardly wait to return and share his experiences with Michelle, but knew there would be many work responsibilities that would need his attention!

CHAPTER 29

When James returned from Egypt, the first thing he did was to call Michelle and arrange a date with her. James knew that there were three things that Michelle enjoyed and one of them was dining out at one of the restaurants they liked and another was shopping for clothes and shoes… and still another was dancing on the beach under a full moon. Since there was only just a new moon, James decided on the former two things.

First, James took Michelle shopping for high heel shoes. Although this was a laborious process because Michelle liked to try on many different styles and kept changing her mind about what she wanted, it made her happy. Therefore James let it make him happy; albeit, picking out shoes would not be something that James would choose to do. After Michelle had finally picked out a pair of high heel shoes and James paid for them, he could see Michelle smiling and light radiated from around her head as if she had been doing Tai Chi… except that she was Tai shopping!

So for brunch, James took Michelle to the Velvet Turtle champagne brunch, which was "their place" for such events—such a variety of very tasty foods. James marveled at the way Michelle beamed and radiated light—like the light from her aura when she was happy and the Velvet Turtle made her happy. James commented about this, telling Michelle, "It really makes me happy to see you so happy. You know, Michelle, what I learned and experienced in Egypt really makes me happy because of the several incredible things happened, which I related to you on the phone."

Michelle, responded, "I can see something powerful happened to you in Egypt. You are more confident and more than the aura of confidence, you are radiating light like the Sun."

"Well," James replied, "I found more information and experiences related to 'The Hidden Codes of God.' Every time I have discovered these things, it has changed me. Even though some of these things are not directly related to Christian Science, they all tie together and they enhance each other. I kind of had a living proof of reincarnation while walking through the Temple of Luxor. But when I went into a state of bliss where my breathing and heart stopped in the King's Chamber, I began to sense the immortality of life and experience God in such a profound manner that it is hard to put into words. But I can say that when your body is in a highly activated state of energy and light, you can more profoundly experience God—exactly why, I am not sure! And yet as I think about it, I am figuring it out. Since God is pure energy, when we approach that state of being-ness, we are in a more complete and sympathetic resonance with the Creator. Yes, it must be related to energy field resonance."

"Wow!" Michelle exclaimed. "You are really on a roll and I am not talking about those delicious sweet rolls either. By experiencing these things you were able to get tremendous insights into them and then you pieced together their significance and importance."

"Exactly!" James exclaimed. "And it all relates or interrelates with sexuality."

"Well I knew I could count on you to bring up sexuality." Michelle replied. "And yet I, too, can see how these things are interrelated."

"I am so glad," James replied, "because for me this is all so, so, so self evident!" "When my breathing and heart stopped," James explained, "I was completely free of the limitations of my body. But the most amazing thing was that my heart was completely open and I was enveloped in an intense field of love, akin to what happens when we sexually conjoin our energies."

"So you are saying you do not need sex anymore?" Michelle queried.

"No," James exclaimed in exasperation, "I am only relating this incredible thing that happened to me. I so enjoy being intimate with you—it is incredibly transcendent and liberating. You know I adore the crap out of you, Michelle. I sometimes wonder if you really appreciate that."

Michelle pondered what James said to her and replied, "Yes I know you adore me but sometimes I feel it is too much—like you are smothering me. Sometimes I need my space when you want to be intimate with me. I feel like I am losing my independence."

James then replied, "Is not that the ultimate goal—giving up our independence and merging with the Creator? I feel we approach this merging with God during an intense sexual experience, do you not agree, Michelle?"

"I don't think I experience things as intensely or completely as you, James," Michelle responded.

As their relationship continued, this differing viewpoint became a point of contention between James and Michelle;

James being very addicted to Michelle and her wiles and Michelle being more circumspect and at times shunning or disdainful of intimacy. James was sure that if he were patient with Michelle, her attitude would change. But he also knew that he would have to muster tremendous patience to accomplish this. Rather than overly focus on this issue, James just decided to be in the moment with Michelle and enjoy her presence. He knew that after shopping and a good meal, Michelle would be open to and desirous of sexual intimacy with James and that it would only be a matter of time before Michelle would be amenable to his sexual advances. And in fact this is just what occurred and in a quick fashion, so much so that they got a hotel room instead of taking the time to go to one of their residences. James found his sexual conjoining with Michelle very exciting and liberating and could not contemplate how Michelle could feel anything else!

CHAPTER 30

What James had failed to realize about Michelle's on again off again attitude toward romantic relationships was that she carried many painful experiences from her childhood and past lifetimes. She would talk to James about these things: how mean her mother was and how nice her father, a petroleum engineer, was, but also how he did not protect his children from their mother. So with all of this lodged in Michelle's subconscious, it made her suspicious of the intentions of people, especially in a romantic relationship.

And the irony of all of this was that Michelle was a very open hearted individual. She had a lot of empathy for anyone who needed help and would not hesitate to try to help them. James witnessed this many times with his own eyes, but every time he tried to take his romantic relationship with Michelle to the next level of intimacy and trust, she would find some reason or excuse not progress further.

Michelle would tell James that she wanted to be married, which is why James divorced Ann. But after the divorce was finalized, Michelle started vacillating on her marriage intentions. One week he would be able to be close to Michelle and the next week she made excuses why she could not spend time with him. This yo-yo relationship started taking its toll on James, but not necessarily so much Michelle. So James started getting interested in another, older woman who was subtly and aggressively pursuing him. This older woman, Annette, was giving James ample hints that things would never work out with Michelle. Annette had a lot of psychic ability and insights and had expertise in astrology. But her information might have been tinged by the fact that she was very attracted to Scorpio's, especially those born on Halloween. She would keep mentioning to James that he needed to be with someone who he could depend on, subtly implying that Michelle was unreliable as a mate. In fact, Annette was correct in her allegations.

And eventually, due to Michelle's reticence to proceed down the path to marriage, James began a torrid relationship with Annette. The fact that she was twelve years older than James was inconsequential to him. What was important was that she was beautiful and sensual and open hearted, and… she could not get pregnant, due to having a hysterectomy. Despite the fact that the energy James and Annette created through their sexual escapades was incredibly manifested and they were sexually compatible, James felt that something was missing—an element that he had with Michelle and his two Ann's.

So when Michelle, who was jealous of James' relationship with Annette, suggested that they get back together as a couple, James could not resist her wiles. Michelle, wanting to make James feel he had made the right decision, pushed herself to new levels of intimacy with him the night of their reunion. As the energy was building between them during their foreplay, James exclaimed, "Michelle, I feel that you are really letting yourself go and following your heart with no reservations. Why would you not have done this sooner? I am so intoxicated with your presence, including your beautiful face and ass and breasts that I am beside myself. I feel that you are finally ready to become my wife."

Michelle replied, "I really missed you James but I worry that you love me more than I love you. You want to have sex all the time whereas I really only need it occasionally."

After they both had mind shattering orgasms, they laid delirious in the arms of each other they stroked each other and laid on the bed in contentment just beaming and glowing with delight at the intense energy that had been created between them. Then James exclaimed, "Why would you not want to have sex all the time considering what we can create between us? Can you deny that what we have is special beyond all description and would make other couples envious of what we have? Can you deny that we enter the level of divine perfection when we join ourselves together?"

Michelle, shook her head yes and yet James sensed they still were not on the same page. "God, this is hard," he exclaimed, "I just love the shit out of you Michelle. You really get to me—you really transport me to a oneness with the Divine!"

Michelle just shrugged and said, "You are just so intense that it scares me sometimes. You are surer about things than I am. In every relationship with a man I have ever been with, I have always had lots problems. So it always lingers in the back of my head and I cannot have the same certainty about things that you have!"

"Yet you can make the decision to trust in what we have created to allow yourself to break through this," James replied. "Remember all those patterns of unworthiness to have things that we removed in the Tibetan Foundation?" James continued.

"Yes," Michelle replied, "we removed a ton of crap but there still must be more." So with this as a backdrop, the relationship languished in the area of uncertainty with James being very certain that it was mutually beneficial and Michelle conflicted with lingering doubt.

"You know," James exclaimed, "that we have been privileged to be experiencing things from "The Hidden Codes of God" that have been obscured from humanity. Ninety-nine plus percent of the populace on Earth have never known or experienced these things, so we are literally pioneers in this field of divine knowledge."

"Yes," Michelle replied, "I know you are right but I am apparently not able to move as fast as you into this. You need to have patience with me, James. If I did not love you I would not be with you. Can you comprehend that?"

"I can understand what you are saying," James responded, "I just know we would both benefit from trusting what we have created and taking full advantage of it. It is so frustrating that you cannot seize this opportunity on a deeper level."

Well, things were really churned up when Michelle invited her ex-boyfriend, Chui, to come to her house when he was doing trance channeling of entities for a small group of friends. Chui arrived late for the gathering and up until that time things were going fine. When Chui showed up with one of his students, he started asking James questions about his life and did not like and/or agree with the answers that were provided. He became very violent physically and struck James several times in the head.

James, being a master of Tai Chi, relaxed through these blows and was completely unharmed. Once again Chui unloaded a barrage of strikes to James' body with no damage done thereto. This quite astonished Chui since he was a Southeast Asian Karate champion in his weight class. Eventually the police arrived after a call from a neighbor reporting that Chui was audibly yelling threats to kill James. With the Tai Chi connection, James was demonstrating to himself that a practitioner of Tai Chi could always be protected from anything, while circulating massive amounts of chi/ prāṇa/life force throughout the body—basically in a 24/7 field of protection from the various onslaughts encountered in life!

The police arrested Chui; Michelle begged James to have the assault and battery charges dropped against him, because she was afraid Chui would eventually attack her also if he was convicted. James had a lot of reservation about doing this, but did so in the light of knowing that he had been very violent at times in his life and so possibly he should cut Chui some slack since his own behavior had been marginal at times also.

So with the event with Chui, and the reality of Michelle possibly never taking their relationship to its ultimate level staring James in the face, he was open to taking a different path in his life. James decided to participate in a "Sage Experience" encounter group for a weekend and had hopes of meeting another girlfriend. Chui seemed to be under the impression that he was Michelle's common law husband since they had co-habited for more than seven years. James really

Robert J. Newton, J.D., N.D

did not want to deal with all of this drama, even though he adored Michelle immensely!

CHAPTER 31

The Sage Experience was an encounter group format where every participant faced the flaws in their personalities and were taught to recognize the faults they saw in others as possible faults in themselves. James dove headfirst into this experiential seminar. Basically, it was a mirroring phenomenon and an intense one at that! Although this was a very intimidating way to be confronted, James quickly saw the usefulness and embraced it.

This technique made it easier to forgive flaws in parents, siblings, and friends, and in romantic relationships. James could see how this "Sage Experience" could be part of the hidden codes in that it allowed a person to quickly change their perception about people and things. And thus, it allowed a person to be powerful and quickly evolve, which was in conjunction with everything James had previously learned about "The Hidden Codes of God." It was a resolution protocol that allowed people to let go of the past, among other things.

There were several women whom James felt were attractive, in one way or another, who participated in the "Sage Experience." There were more beautiful women James could have chosen to link up with other than Lisette, but he felt that she could be a kindred spirit, so he asked her out on a group date. She had chosen a spiritual path and was pursing a spiritual life beyond orthodox religion. On their first date, Lisette said, "I want you to come home with me and stay the night in my bed but I do not want to have sex! Are you amendable to this?"

"James replied, "Of course it is ok since my experience has been that if you do not rush into a sexual encounter at the very beginning of a relationship, it will usually last for a lot longer and be more satisfying, likewise." So the couple went to Lisette's apartment and quickly in bed with each other, in only their underwear. They cuddled and kissed and engaged in a significant amount of heavy petting; James passionately caressed Lisette and she responded in kind.

Then Lisette took off her underwear and got back into bed and began to stroke James' penis. At that point, Lisette spread her legs, inviting James with this signal to enter her vagina. So in the heat of passion—totally immersed in the moment—James thrust his penis into Lisette and thought it was interesting how things were working out. James was focusing on the task ahead—creating tremendous energy between himself and Lisette. But he sensed that she was crying. So James asked Lisette, "Have I done something wrong? I thought you wanted to have sex! Why are you crying?"

Lisette replied, "It is not you, but rather I am so sad about the fact that my relationship with my recent boyfriend ended and I cared so much about him. Apparently he was not as enamored with me as I was with him."

James responded, "I can identify with that since I just left a relationship with the same dynamics, myself."

Lisette said, "I thought that by having sex with you, it would wipe out the memory of my old boyfriend but it is not working."

Upon hearing her comment, James withdrew his penis from Lisette's vagina and just held and cuddled and kissed her for much of the remaining night. In the morning, Lisette told James, "I am so glad you were understanding of my predicament. There are not many men who would even care about my plight. They would just keep humping away until they exploded with an orgasm. What you did meant so much to me I will reward you tomorrow night."

"Well," James replied, "I guess compassion and understanding do generate their own reward. But I do not want to rush you into anything for which you are not sure you are ready!"

"Actually," Lisette responded, "your tenderness and understanding and compassion with me allowed me to let go of my old relationship… so you helped to set me free of my old boyfriend. I want to move forward with you!"

So that next night, Lisette displayed a compelling and seductive form that attracted James in a very ethereal manner. As they were watching television at Lisette's apartment, she sat in James' lap at times smoking a cigarette. While James really did not like the smoke from the cigarettes, he chose to ignore it as much as possible and become enthralled with the subtle aspects of Lisette. While they were joined together sitting in the chair, James became quite energized and his penis became very stiff and he circulated a lot of chi throughout his body as well as his penis. This just made James want to kiss and caress Lisette and they both became excited, even if in a somewhat controlled manner. So after watching television, they hurried off to Lisette's bedroom and quickly removed each other's clothes.

But James still took his time before he even thought about penetrating Lisette's vagina with his penis. He began kissing her inner thighs, not even bothering to suck and caress her feet because he could read that she was more than ready for penetration. After kissing her inner thighs, James worked up to Lisette's vagina and began to drive her wild with his tongue darting about and repeatedly stimulating her clitoris. She was so turned on that she had an orgasm, which flowed the juices into his mouth that James so adored. James was literally addicted to this vaginal odor and it served to turn him on even more.

Eventually, Lisette begged James to penetrate her with his penis and he obliged her, as he was aroused almost beyond control. Once James had entered the "cave of love," he had to tighten his anal sphincter muscles because he did not want to prematurely ejaculate; he wanted Lisette to have another orgasm. As he could feel her approaching the threshold of orgasmic delight, James began to allow himself to prepare for ejaculation, but he kept his anal sphincter muscles contracted to intensify his orgasm. As Lisette began to orgasm, James allowed himself to release his sperm and share his chi/life force with her. They were both rewarded with thunderous orgasms, which synchronized with each other, thus intensifying everything as they played off the tremendous energy they released and shared. "Wow," James exclaimed, "that was worth the wait. What we shared was very special and memorable! The kind of energy we created is very rare and special and rarely ever experienced by lovers on this planet. With you in my arms, I cannot really tell where I end and you begin, Lisette. I could really get addicted to being with you!"

"Well I think you have healed me," Lisette replied, kind of like Marvin Gaye's *Sexual Healing* song. Would you second that James?" James nodded his head in agreement and a huge smile covered his face as he burst out into uncontrollable laughing.

"What's not to be happy about?" James exclaimed in in forceful manner! "Yes, we have been healed!"

James and Lisette languished in the energy they created. It produced a relaxation that is hard to describe, but it was like everything slowed down, as if a trance state of enlightenment was being attained. And what James learned from this trancelike state was that not only could sexual conjoining create huge amounts of energy, but it could also aid in certain transcendence through negative emotions and energies. But would this have lasting effects for Lisette, or would it be temporary?

That question would be soon answered for James. Lisette displayed a take-it-or-leave-it attitude in general, about their relationship, in that she really did not want to commit herself to a dedicated one. She also made numerous comments that they should keep their relationship casual with little expectations from each other. James could only conclude that Lisette was trying to protect herself from being hurt in another relationship as she was with her previous boyfriend. So in Lisette's case, James realized that her "sexual healing" was merely a temporary thing and not something with long lasting effects. Once again, James was faced being in a relationship, such as with Michelle, where one partner was unable to commit fully enough to journey into new territory—into the unknown wherein a person can experience

"The Hidden Codes of God," and all the beneficial results related thereto!

Although the sex between James and Lisette was intense and satisfying, James knew that he could never go with Lisette where he had gone with both of his Ann's. It just would never happen until those emotional hurts—the deep wounds—were dealt with sufficiently to eliminate them from Lisette's subconscious. And James began to learn from listening to Lisette talk about her life, that her father was as much as responsible for Lisette's emotional trauma as much as her previous boyfriend. James began to sense that Lisette's damaged relationship with her father caused her problems with her boyfriend, as well as the lack of commitment to him. James did not like this turn of events, but he understood them because of his unhappy childhood experiences, which were many. But he also knew that he would ultimately evolve and become more enlightened by having a romantic partner who could fearlessly commit to going forward into the unknown; James knew that there were more hidden codes that could be revealed to him! Whether James had become a Sage from the "Sage Experience," he was uncertain. But he was certain the experience taught him a lot about himself and a few more aspects of "The Hidden Codes of God."

CHAPTER 32

James knew it was time to continue his quest for the hidden codes with another partner. And it so happened that his friend, Severn, who co-led a meditation group with James, said he had an ex-girlfriend, Lynn, who he thought would mesh with him. She lived on the East Coast… a continent apart from James' home in the Los Angeles area. But James took the initiative and called her and conversed with her and found they had much in common. And because sleeping under a large holographic pyramid had enhanced his intuition, James could pick up things about Lynn that were not communicated verbally. Lynn complained her current boyfriend, who already had a wife, would not divorce his wife and marry her, and she had broken up with him.

James found this to be a fortuitous event and after hours of conversation with Lynn, he told her that he was going to fly to South Carolina to meet her. She was kind of stunned that James would do this but also extremely happy because the relationship she had just left was not working. Her married boyfriend just could not give her enough time. And James was likewise excited since he had not even seen a picture of Lynn, and wanted to test the psychic impressions he was receiving.

The day James flew into South Carolina to see Lynn, there was great anticipation of just what would happen when he met her. Upon disembarking from the plane, James saw this mysterious looking woman and he knew it was Lynn. As he approached her, Lynn came up to him and said, "Welcome, my long lost lover!" And then she put her arms around his neck and looked into his eyes and gave him a passionate kiss that more than got James' attention and definitely excited him. Lynn said, "I am anxious to take you to my apartment—are you ready?"

And James just smiled at her and replied, "Why would I not be ready? I have been most anxious to meet you. I know we have been together in a previous lifetime. I am so attracted to you and I am so glad that I just followed my intuition about you and made this trip here to meet you! So, yes, let's go to your apartment!"

After about a twenty-minute drive from the Columbia, South Carolina Airport, they arrived at Lynn's apartment. As soon as they entered Lynn's apartment, she hurriedly removed her clothes and pulled James onto her bed and began kissing him torridly. James asked her. "Are you sure you do not want to get to know me better before we proceed any further?"

"No, this is exactly what I want to do. I am so grateful that you came to see me and I am going to reward you for your efforts. I know everything about you from the Tarot card readings I have done on you," Lynn explained.

"Well," James replied, "your wish is my command because I am so damn happy to meet a woman as open hearted and passionate as you."

"Then please," Lynn begged, "get to the task at hand."

James did not need any more prodding although the scenario brought back thoughts of other failed relationships where the immediate progression to sexual coupling led to short lived relationships. But by the time these thoughts found their way to James' consciousness, it was probably past the point of no return since Lynn's passion was overwhelming James with the most incredibly powerful feminine energy imaginable—unlike any other he had previously experienced. And all of this energy came in a package with a beautiful face and a lean yet curvaceous body! So James just let himself flow into the circumstances of the immediate situation and he ravaged Lynn's body and face, which brought her to an even higher output of Divine Energy and in the process, he was likewise transported to higher levels of energy and consciousness.

James asked Lynn, "Please tell anything that you want me to do to you that I might not be doing but that you would enjoy!"

Lynn just responded, "Everything is fantastic. It blows me away that you know just exactly what I need to be transported to heaven. Is there anything you need from me?"

"Well," James replied, "I would really like to have anal sex with you."

Lynn quickly replied, "Be my guest. You must really want to love the shit out of me, right?

"Well," James exclaimed, "you could say no holes barred. But really I am throwing all caution to the wind since you are exciting and prodding me to greater heights of surrender to your feminine presence."

Lynn just reminded James, "Please wash your penis off before you visit my vagina!"

"Of course," James exclaimed. "From a hygienic perspective, that is necessary. I brought some hydrogen peroxide with me and I will do just that!"

And so James proceeded with his anal sex with Lynn and it definitely drove her wild, so much so that she had a powerful orgasm. Before he moved to her vagina, he did in fact wash his penis with hydrogen peroxide, dried it and then made his move to the conventional tunnel of love. By this time, since they were both in such an aroused sexual state, the energy created between them literally fused them into one cohesive unit. There was already so much energy coursing up and down their spines and accumulating in their heads, that they both knew their impending orgasms would push them past their existing boundary of consciousness. Each deliberately delayed their orgasm through anal bandam locks, but eventually they both erupted with massive volcano-like orgasms that were simultaneously achieved!

James was so deep into trance level consciousness he was just doing things instinctively. He took Lynn in his arms and hugged her strongly and kissed her all over her body; Lynn responded in kind. James wanted to be fused with Lynn as long as possible. And he wished his penis would never go soft since he wanted to be inside Lynn's vagina for as long as possible. Both Lynn and James knew they were enveloped in a Divine Energy that could not really be adequately described, but sure could be experienced, as they were so doing… in a state of divine ecstasy!

After some time, Lynn exclaimed, "I really enjoyed it when you entered my ass. When you were probing me in the anus, I was so turned on. At first I just thought your idea was so weird but I quickly realized you were quite creative and uninhibited and I just went with your wish and direction."

"I had this feeling you would like this, and I didn't even have a Tarot card spread! One of my girlfriends begged me to have anal sex with her because she could not orgasm vaginally. So I did what she asked and she exploded into a powerful orgasm and it turned me on likewise." "At first, I had strong reservations about doing this because I heard anal sex reversed the polarity energies and lowered a person's vibration, until I realized that I could control the polarity and vibration through my mental intent."

The weekend of James' visit went as well as could possibly be expected. The two repeated amazing sexual chemistry and energy and James could not imagine how things could be more intensely and divinely experienced. He reached a state of relaxation that only helped to facilitate the intensity and circulation of life force energies throughout his body. The only thing that he saw as a problem was Lynn's propensity to do Tarot card spreads to read things about him. Several times Lynn stated, "You are hiding things from me James... what is that you are hiding?"

And James promptly replied, "I am hiding nothing. What do you want to know and what do you think I am hiding?"

"I cannot exactly tell," Lynn responded, "but I am sure there is something!"

And James quietly responded, "There is nothing I am hiding... I have no hidden agenda nor campaigns of deceit and you can be sure of that! You could just be over analyzing things and I have found it all too often breaks up relationships... and I mean that literally."

The weekend came to a close and James had to return to Southern California to tend to his landscaping and construction business, but he kept in daily contact with Lynn, either by phone or telepathically and usually both. James was looking forward to taking Lynn to Hawaii as they had planned during a conversation they had in Charleston. James found Charleston magical and romantic, but Lynn, never having gone to Hawaii before, was very excited about going there.

She complained, "My ex-boyfriend was always going there but he never ever took me along."

James replied, "Pretty crappy boyfriend if you ask me, but his loss is my gain because I am going to take you to my favorite spots in Maui and you will feel the powerful feminine energy that envelops the entire island and I know you will be blown away by it all."

Once Lynn arrived in California, the couple embarked to Hawaii, leaving via L.A. International Airport. They landed in Honolulu and due to a mistake in checking their baggage; James became very irritated at himself since it would not arrive with them on their shuttle flight to Maui.

Lynn couldn't understand why James was so upset. He explained that they would waste time going back to the airport to get their baggage, after their arrival and in frustration said, "I am here to relax and explore this beautiful country and that did not include searching for our baggage!"

Anyway, when they arrived and deplaned, Lynn finally commented on what James told her about the feminine energy that surrounded Maui. "Wow James," she said, "you really are not exaggerating and if anything, you more fully

166

understated the pervasive feminine presence here. I remember you telling me that there was a civilization here about 300,000 years ago called Lemuria and that the Lemurians were a peaceful people; very spiritual with highly developed psychic abilities and basically communicated telepathically."

"That is all correct as far as I can ascertain," James said. "It is so mellow here it just seems that it is easier to read someone else's thoughts. I can tell you that I feel very romantic when I visit this place. One of my girlfriends would not come here with me because she feared I would be too amorous," James explained.

"That is ridiculous and you will not have to worry about that with me," Lynn proclaimed.

"Good," James replied, "Because I think this place is the key to understanding and experiencing 'The Hidden Codes of God' and I know romance is a portal thereto. It certainly is not the only way, but it certainly is a valid and very enjoyable way to accomplished it and is hard for me to understand why anyone would not want to do it this way," James continued.

"There is this discipline," James related, "called brahmachari, which says that spiritual enlightenment can only come through chastity. This comes from Hinduism and Yoga and probably other religions also. And yet within this same Hindu tradition is the discipline of Tantra, and in China, Taoism… they are both devoted to using the sexual energies to transport a person's consciousness into a state of transcendence. Truly the Tantric and Taoist disciplines can do just what they claim and most people who practice this concept of chastity find it difficult and frustrating to follow.

So I would say, duh, if this is so difficult to follow it must not be natural or divine!"

Lynn curtly replied, "Duh, in my own estimation, you are correct-a-mundo, James!"

The hotel where they stayed was south of Kaanapali Beach, at Makena Shores; isolated from other hotels with its own very wide and sandy beach, it was certainly suited for long romantic walks, which is just what they did. As James and Lynn walked along the beach, hand in hand, and kissing each other with regularity, the life force energy of love overtook them in a most sensual and exciting way. Their sensuality created a feeling of extreme relaxation that was compounded by the natural energy of love that surrounded Maui. And their relaxation allowed more of this pranic energy/life force to enter into their bodies, which excited them even more.

As they were returning to their hotel room, James said, "When we get back to the hotel room I have a present I think you will really like."

"Please tell me what it is," Lynn begged.

James just said, "You will find out soon enough."

When they got back to the room Lynn asked, "Where is my present?" To which James replied, "I am the present and the present is that I am going to withhold my orgasm for a long time until you have first had many consecutive orgasms yourself."

"Are you sure you can really deliver that James," Lynn replied.

"Oh, yeah, I am positive I can do that. Maui and its energy field has relaxed me so much that it will be easy to achieve!" James exclaimed.

The couple shed their swim wear, and James took Lynn in his arms and pulled her down to the bed with her on top as he landed on his back. James felt so much energy coming from Lynn's heart—compounded by the Maui love energy field—that life force energy/electricity was powerfully coursing through his body and he could no longer feel his body… only the energy of the electricity. He shared the feelings emanating from his heart with Lynn as he caressed, kissed and fondled her. Pretty soon, the walls of the hotel seemed to melt away in a sense that they no longer appeared solid. James could care less about the walls were solid or not as it appeared to him that Lynn was also deep into a trance; her eyes having a far away look and turned upward as though lost to the world and unconcerned about anything. James would soon learn just how significant the upward look of the eyes was as he and Ann studied more about the discipline of Kriya Kundalini Pranayama's (yoga) and description of theta consciousness/trance consciousness!

For now, James was only concerned about fulfilling his promise to Lynn and this was only going to be possible if he was successful in creating a very strong anal sphincter lock (also known as a bandam lock). It was easier to accomplish with Lynn on top of him and would have been even easier to do having sex in the Dog or Tortoise position, but for whatever reason Lynn on top was his choice. Lynn went to a 69 position wherein she had James penis in her mouth and he was probing her vagina with his tongue. As enjoyable as the position was for James, he finally directed Lynn to switch her orientation so that her head was united with his. When Lynn shifted, James entered her vagina with his penis and began to move it in and out, but in a controlled and slow manner. Then, with Lynn on top of him, James arched his back to the extreme and continued to thrust into her. The new position helped James create his desired anal bandam root lock and it was not long before Lynn was moaning in delight as she approached her first orgasm. When she finally exploded into her orgasm, James had a great look of satisfaction on his face, but not nearly as much satisfaction as was displayed over Lynn's.

Fortunately, Lynn did not have much time for the satisfied look because in a few minutes she was on the threshold of her next orgasm; James knew it was imminent by the way she was moaning. His lovemaking took great concentration of James' part to prevent his orgasm. He was successful in preventing it and Lynn, unaware of James' extended efforts, erupted into a second orgasm. After her second climax, James was able to assert more control over his ejaculation and Lynn proceeded to have at least eight more orgasms.

After the tenth one, Lynn said, "Baby, you are driving me wild. I have never experienced anything like this. You are amazing and it scares me the power you have over me."

James replied, "I do not wish to have power over you but only to push you deeply into the energy of Love which pervasively emanates from our Creator."

"Well whatever you are doing, James, I have never experienced before and I have never even read of such delight being experienced by anyone," Lynn proclaimed.

"Nor have I," James replied.

Ultimately, James had controlled the delay of his orgasm so well that when he decided it was his turn to orgasm, it was actually difficult to initiate the process. But with Lynn humping up and down on him, he finally reached a simultaneous orgasm with her. With all the energy she shared with James, he got an idea of the scope of what Lynn had and was experiencing. It was truly disorienting and he was aware they obviously had both been transported into a higher dimension of energy—where the illusion of matter no longer existed—because everything was ethereal looking with no hard definition to objects such as walls and beds and people, specifically Lynn. The couple continued to bask in these higher dimensions of love for many hours after.

James shared his thoughts with Lynn when he exclaimed, "This is actual proof of 'The Hidden Codes of God' not only in fact but in actual operation that can be visually and viscerally experienced! For me, this is more than just an intense event—it actually is revelatory because I can see the theory in action as you can likewise, Lynn."

"I really can't deny what you are saying, because I see it myself," Lynn responded. "You know, it is rather like heaven on Earth, James."

James agreed with a nod of his head and said, "This is exactly what Mary Baker Eddy wrote in *Science and Health with Key to the Scriptures,* where she explicitly stated that heaven could be experienced by us while we are here on Earth. It appears she knew exactly what she was talking about and now I see it so clearly; before it was only a remote concept which I knew was true but had never seen such a thing in operation.

This is just so damn cool and beyond! Who would believe this if we told them these things, Lynn? Mrs. Eddy really tuned into the hidden codes."

James continued, "With my first true love, Ann, I experienced a lot of skepticism and doubt when we shared that sexual conjoining could actually transport us to the realm of spirit-energy. We never even talked about other dimensions, yet now I can see we experienced even that. Those experiences were over twenty years ago, and I still have doubts humanity, in general, is ready for these insights. I guess I will have to write a book about it. I have been thinking about a book called, *Pathways to God: Experiencing the Living God in Your Everyday Life*. Do you think I can pull that off, Lynn?'

"I would say you are extremely qualified to write the book. The "proof in the pudding" is what we just created." Lynn exclaimed.

"I guess so." James replied. "But for now I just want to experience your energy… and the energy we attracted into our lives. God has greatly blessed us by sharing His presence with us, and I feel deeply blessed to share this understanding with you, Lynn."

Lynn coyly smiled at James and said, "Baby, you have done most of the work!"

James just replied, "God was doing the work because the Creator must energize and perpetuate everything or we cease to exist in animate form. I feel your presence so deeply inside of me that it is hard to truly appreciate or communicate the depths of those feelings to you, but I know you know that I know what I am trying to say and I know that you feel it likewise!"

After several hours of just letting the emotionally derived higher dimensional energy penetrate their bodies and being taken to a state of ecstasy, both James and Lynn decided to take a walk on the beach under the backing of a full moon. It was like they were almost floating over the sand and actually seemed as they though their feet barely made an impression in the sand. James then said to Lynn, "Now I guess you truly understand why I feel Maui is just so magical and full of love!"

After a few quiet moments of her own Lynn replied, "What do you mean, you guess I understand the love power of Maui? I would have to be discarnate not to understand and experience all of this, James!"

"Well," James replied, I did not want to be accused of hyperbolic statements, but I guess there is not much chance of exaggerating things about this place, is there?"

"That is pretty impossible," Lynn responded.

The gravitational effects of the moon had a spell binding effect on James and Lynn's already altered perception of things and the energy catalyzed even more amorous feelings between them. So finally, they went back up to their hotel room and had an encore performance of their previous sexual union. This time James' idea was that he would have multiple orgasms in a short span of time.

Lynn asked, "How do plan on pulling that off, James?"

James just smiled his customary smile, and he then laughed and explained, "You will be pumping up my penis between acts—literally squeezing it repeatedly and it will most likely come to life again. Annette used that move on me and it worked quite amazingly!"

"Do I need a tire pump?" Lynn giggled, and James just rolled his eyes.

"Just follow my lead," James explained, "this time we will conjoin in the dog position and it will make things easier for me but a little more work for you. But, I promise you it will be more than worth the effort. We will be diving back into that same energy field we created earlier in the day!" And that in fact is just what happened: Multiple simultaneous orgasms—and even deeper immersions into the higher dimensions of lovemaking. After three glorious and simultaneous orgasms, it was difficult to even remotely relate to the third dimension. That suited James and Lynn just fine since it was indicative that they were going deeper into the dimension known as Divine Love and all obstacles to opening their hearts symbolically and literally had been eliminated!

The sexual experiences during the rest of the week on Maui were similar to what happened on this day, with variations and experimentation on what could get them highest sexually, but nothing exceeded this day. James would later ponder whether it was possibly because it was the full moon, which he knew to definitely have dimensional stretching properties. James and Lynn visited the Iao Needle, and they could sense a real powerful energy emanating from the natural rock pinnacle that seemed to "preside" over the area, which was filled with energy vortexes and a raging stream.

When the couple returned from Maui and settled in the Los Angeles area, James realized a startling difference in his travel mate's demeanor; she was cold and matter of fact about things and not her usual affectionate self. James was perplexed about what was occurring and confronted Lynn about it; she shrugged it off and just blamed it on menstrual related things. In his heart James knew something else was going on... regardless of Lynn's explanations. He was sad to see her go back home in light of all they had experienced in a short period of time and later found out from Severn that Lynn was upset that James was upset about the luggage scenario, when he hadn't properly booked the bags through to Maui. After all that... James found out from Lynn, over the phone, that she was going to get back with her ex-boyfriend!

James was almost speechless when he heard this round of news; it was his intention to marry her. James boldly asked Lynn, "Did you ever reach the heights of sexual ecstasy with your ex-boyfriend, Danny, that we achieved? Did you not admit to me that that he was an ex-hitman for the CIA? Did you also not share with me Danny said he would never leave his wife and marry you?"

Lynn admitted, "You are right about all of this, I cannot deny but I want to do healing work with him. He has promised to change and he has agreed to find me a place to live closer to him and to pay the rent."

"So I guess you will settle for being his mistress then." James exclaimed. "I would beg you to reconsider this course of action. Not only have we experienced what you never did with Danny—and never will experience with him—you can probably rest assured he will most likely never marry you! We

175

could do at least as awesome healing work as you will do with him and probably even more."

"Do you have an Ascension Chamber as he does?" Lynn asked James. "Have you done healing work like he has done?" she asked."

"Well, as a matter of fact I do and I have! Even though we have not talked about these things, I am well versed in healing and much more than yourself and your new and former ex-boyfriend. That must have been what you were picking up in your Tarot cards, but you could not figure out! I suppose your Tarot cards told you that you would be better off with him than me, huh? I have a magnetic and crystal pad that will rival anything in his so-called Ascension Chamber!" James could not keep the ire from his voice.

"Wow," Lynn exclaimed, "you are really beating me up, aren't you?" James laughed hysterically and then replied, "I am just stating facts that you admitted to. Your process of making decisions is so questionable as to make me wonder if your ex and now new boyfriend has you under a spell, because you told me he had a radionics machine and whether you realize it or not, Lynn, these things are used for more than just healing! Also, I am quite sure you manipulated the results of the Tarot cards with your conscious or subconscious intent. Apparently you have been bamboozled by that notorious Southern charm, (camouflaged B.S.) Danny slathers about! I find it quite astonishing that you are not taking this into account—nor all that we experienced in Maui. We can recreate that over and over... not to mention I adore you and am ready to marry you. I will also give you the respect he never will and I find it more than ironic that when he has some competition that all of a sudden he starts doting on you and buying your favor.

James' diatribe continued... Do you know Danny went so far as to threaten your ex-boyfriend, and my friend Severn, and said that he would 'take care of him'? He yelled and screamed all these things over the telephone; I would opine my episode with the luggage in Maui, which so upset you, really pales in comparison to his ranting and raving and threatening to do bodily harm to someone."

"I do not want to argue with you James," Lynn responded, "but you can come and visit me in Myrtle Beach and we can have our wonderful sexual experiences."

"You must be freaking kidding me!" James replied, "That would really go over well if I was having sex with you and he came over to your house. He would more than likely attempt to kill me. And I would not be surprised if he is working on me in a negative manner with that radionics machine he has. If you ever reconsider this idiotic and destructive path you have chosen with Danny, let me know. It is obvious to me that you do not feel worthy to have an awesome partner in your life and to have true happiness. You will never have this in a sustained way with Danny, regardless of how hard you try to convince yourself. He cares more about possessing and controlling you rather than respecting and loving you!

A quiet came over James as he delivered the last of what was in his heart, "Lynn, I would never wish to diminish you, but your being with Danny will do just that and in time, even you will have to admit the validity of my statements!"

So once again James was dealing with a woman who had issues with her father. In this case, it was the fact that Lynn's father died when she was very young and her subconscious took it as a signal and mental data entry that men are not to be trusted—that they will never be there when you need them. James certainly was not oblivious to the synchronicity he was experiencing with lovers who had male issues and the resulting intimacy phobia reactions! It was a strong pattern; too forceful to ignore! Regardless of the pain and anguish that James experienced from his rejection by Lynn, he was still grateful for experiencing deeper levels of "The Hidden Codes of God." He would keep moving forward on the journey to learn, know and use them, and in his pursuit of romantic bliss, because although he was baffled by what had just occurred, his heart had been irrevocably opened even more!

CHAPTER 33

Severn, James' friend and co-leader of their meditation group, suggested that James might be interested in a co-worker his wife, Candy, worked with at IBM Federal Systems Division; she had and used pyramid complexes such as what James had from Pyradyne. She had already been invited to the group by Candy, and low and behold, when the friend, Elaine, came to the meditation group James realized he was already interested in this little "sparkplug" of a woman. She definitely had a light that emanated from her body and especially her head!

Normally, there were between 8 and 12 participants at the meditation group, but this time it was just Severn and Candy and James and Elaine. As the group meditation began, the participants joined hands and James performed one of his now famous guided meditations. After the group mediation, each member drifted off into a separate and personal state, but remained with hands joined… serving to more easily facilitate deeper and more profound states of meditation and consciousness. During the time span of the meditation, James began to feel a tremendous amount of energy and electricity flowing through his body. This intensity had never previously occurred within this particular meditation group. Its level was truly euphoric and since James knew Elaine was the only new factor present, he could only attribute it to her presence within the group. Everyone else in the group James had experienced multiple times; this energy was significantly different.

At the end of the meditation, James was effusive about what had happened but apparently he was the only one of the group who had this intense experience; he did not care. James was confident what happened was the result of the presence and energy of Elaine, so he asked her to go to a dance at a bar where the group often went after their sessions. Elaine declined even though she was smiling at him a lot. James got her telephone number from Candy, who assured James Elaine was certainly interested in him.

James called Elaine the next day and asked her again to go on a date; this time to a restaurant that night and she gladly accepted his invitation. Elaine shared she too was looking forward to her date with James and that she did not accept his earlier dancing invitation because she already had a date that night. What James would learn later was it was a date with a cocaine dealer and Elaine was a cocaine user! Without this full knowledge, James was quite taken with Elaine and her perky personality. Elaine was likewise dazzled with James, not only because he brought her roses for their first date, but also because his very essence filled her with humor and laughter.

When they were finished with dinner, Elaine invited James back to her apartment and he naturally accepted the offer. When they arrived at Elaine's apartment, she grabbed James around the waist and began hugging him and he responded in kind as he stooped over and began kissing her fleshy, sensual lips. In no time at all, they were both on Elaine's bed and shortly thereafter she removed her top. James began kissing and caressing her ample breasts and tried to get her to remove her skirt because he wanted to have oral sex with her. James was extremely aroused, swimming in the succeeding intense waves of energy that bathed his body and head. Their activities ensued for several hours and eventually the pair fell asleep in each other's arms.

The next day they spent together and that night they went to a movie, *Fatal Attraction*. Although the movie was perverse in parts, other parts were romantically torrid and soon had James very aroused. When they returned to Elaine's apartment, he told her how much he wanted to completely merge with her sexually. She likewise agreed that they should fully consummate their relationship and it did not take much time until James had removed all of Elaine's clothes. Her vaginal juices were really flowing, and James was especially concentrating on stimulating her clitoris with his tongue.

Finally, Elaine asked James, "Are you ready to fuck me with your penis? Do you like doggie style?"

James replied, "Yes, to both questions, but how did you know I liked doggie style?"

Elaine responded, "My ex-husband really enjoyed it and I thought you would too!"

"Well," James exclaimed, "you are right. I really love dog style as it gives me more control over things—specifically, my penis."

James rammed away at Elaine's pussy and he could tell that she was getting excited but then she told him, "I cannot have an orgasm but I want you to blast away because it will make me very happy." That is exactly what James did; he startled Elaine with his screaming when he climaxed and yelled out that he loved her as he was in the midst of his orgasm.

This turned Elaine on more than James could have imagined. But still, for James, there was something missing when his woman did not have an orgasm with him. He was sure that he eventually would get Elaine to climax in some way shape or form. He went down on her for an extended period of time, stimulating her clitoris repeatedly for almost half an hour; still... no orgasm.

Elaine comforted James, "Don't worry about that because it really turned me on when you yelled out that you love me. God, that excited me and made me feel real special."

James really enjoyed the sexual conjoining with Elaine, but unfortunately would discover in a short period of time there was much baggage that came because of her heavy drug usage and alcoholic beverage consumption. As she started sharing the history of her drug and alcohol abuse, it became quite evident to James Elaine basically could not function without the use of some substance or another. But the thing that heartened James was she told him in no uncertain terms she wanted to stop using the mind- altering substances. James thought she was sincere about her claim and was certain he could help Elaine accomplish her goal, using the knowledge and practices he had amassed.

With this information as a backdrop, the relationship proceeded quite quickly and Elaine kept hinting that she wanted James to propose marriage to her. James just laughed and said, "I am sure we will eventually be married." But she kept pressing James about getting married. Finally, James relented and said, "Yes, I will marry you. Let's go down to the

Wholesale Jewelry Mart and get a one carat diamond ring made up for you with a channel of small amethyst quartz stones in the shape of a heart." James' creativity really blew Elaine away because she was unaware that he had considerable experience in lapidary and jewelry making.

But then she asked, "What about a ring for you, James?"

He replied, "I really don't wear rings because I tend to destroy or damage them rather quickly." But finally he relented to Elaine and told her, "Ok, my ring will be the inverse of yours, then. It will have large amethyst quartz in the middle with the channel of diamonds in a heart form surrounding it.

There were other things James and Elaine subsequently found themselves confronted with. Elaine's temporary assignment with IBM would be ending and she would have to move back to her condo in Virginia. "What are we going to do about that, James? Will you move back with me to Virginia?"

It didn't really take James all that long to reply, "Yeah, I have no problem with that since I was thinking of moving of to the state of Washington or Oregon before I met you. So now I will just move close to the Capitol in Washington D.C. instead!"

James had retained both his thriving landscaping and construction companies, and had to leave them behind in California and rebuild a new company in Virginia... using a new plant palette. He had to adjust quickly to a new area and climate zone, a new culture and a lot of unfamiliar plants and trees, but the fact that James had learned to go into a deep meditative state and absorb a lot of information just thereafter, made his new work environment a smoother and easier transition. In the end, James could hit the ground running, except that it was winter in Virginia and not much happened there in landscaping or construction until spring.

Elaine returned to her job at IBM Federal Systems and the couple planned their wedding. Elaine's uncle was a General in the U.S. Army; they were able to have their wedding, without charge, at Fort Belvoir, an army installation center that originally was the site of the Belvoir plantation. The base was vastly more aesthetic than any other James had seen previously; designed by her uncle Bob, who was the General at Fort Belvoir. The General had inside connections, which made the logistics at their wedding go smoother. Unfortunately, the "logistics" of Elaine's life were being disorganized by her continued usage of drugs and alcohol. James was to learn she was under the influence throughout the wedding ceremony and reception. James wasn't aware of this fact earlier and would have been highly angered if he had known. What he was aware of was her substance abuse problems, and he was confident that using the information he had learned (and lived) from the hidden codes would allow him remove all need for drugs and alcohol from her life.

James based his outlook on the fact that he had pulled himself from depression through his first contact with "The Hidden Codes of God." Fortunately, the wedding ceremony occurred without any major hitches, although it is unlikely that Elaine remembered much due to significant drug ingestion.

She would certainly need the wedding pictures and video to remember her own wedding. Apparently, this was why

Elaine was so insistent of having many pictures and videos made of the wedding!

James was the ultimate neophyte to the world of substance abuse, although he would quickly become more educated. The education, however, would be costly—not so much in dollars—but in the frustration and disappointment associated with it.

The happy couple traveled to Colorado for a week to ski many different ski resorts for the first part of their honeymoon. Several days into the week, they went to Vail, Colorado to ski for the day. At lunch, Elaine tried to convince James to have a ski instructor make a video of their skiing. James didn't have any work lined up in Virginia and since they were going to Hawaii for the second week of their honeymoon, he really did not want to spend any more money than he had budgeted… which already added up to many thousands of dollars.

Upon being unsuccessful in persuading James to spend money for the video, Elaine launched into a very loud and vulgar tirade about how cheap James was being. She was relentless for several minutes, exhibiting her emotions in the middle of the chalet; James finally relented.

Being filmed made Elaine quite elated—at least for a while. She was happy and kissed James as she effusively thanked him. James, on the other hand, would have been immensely happier if Elaine's happiness had at least lasted through the evening. Unfortunately this was not to occur. Elaine drank very heavily during their dinner at a restaurant in Vail and by the time the honeymooners finished their meal, Elaine was extremely drunk. She stumbled to the car with

James and they began the ride back to their hotel, an hour away! Along the way, Elaine went into another tirade in the car, swearing at James and calling him a cheap asshole, a motherfucker, and unfortunately... an assortment of other insulting names. Shortly after her outburst, Elaine vomited all over the front seat and then passed out.

When the car arrived at the hotel, Elaine was still passed out and she seemed to be about twice her normal weight. Rather than carrying her up to the hotel room on an upper floor, James put her on a luggage cart to transport her to their room. In the morning, Elaine woke up not knowing what had happened the night before and quite surprised to still be in her ski clothes... and with puke on her ski bibs. From this point forward, James knew that his relationship with Elaine would be full of chaos. In fact, he now understood he should have realized it before the wedding, because he certainly was given enough clues, many of which he ignored.

The rest of the ski honeymoon occurred with less drama but there was always the possibility of drama de jour living with a bi-polar personality. As soon as the Colorado trip came to an end, Elaine and James boarded a plane for Kauai. The energy on the beautiful Hawaiian island seemed to smooth out Elaine's mood swings. With this energetic assistance from nature, James saw the potential in Elaine to able to transcend her bi-polar tendencies and substance addictions. The time in Maui, Hawaii, really softened Elaine and yet she still had to buy her substances, mostly cannabis, which she was able to find at the park in Lahaina... one of Maui's historic towns, since transformed into a Maui hot spot, where, in addition to feeding Elaine's "fix," the couple were able to enjoy dozens of art galleries, unique shops and restaurants. All the while, James' mind reeled with a strong commitment to help his wife face and overcome her demons; he tried to set a sober example and suggested ways in which addiction could be overcome.

James had Elaine try his "brain tuner" an electrical device that had two probes that fit into the soft spot behind the ear. The device put out an alpha brainwave frequency of 7.83 Hertz, which caused an electrical pulse to be sent just behind the ear, and produce a state of meditation. In fact, James knew of several rock stars with drug addiction that had used the technique to overcome their destructive habits. Elaine tried it but just didn't like the discomforting electrical shock that emitted behind her ears. Then James taught her the Tai Chi "Standing Meditation," which she did like. Yet her practice thereof was sporadic, at best, even though James instructed Elaine that it should be done at least once daily, which rarely happened. James was used to people ignoring the glory of the hidden codes but found it hard to grasp his wife's rejecting them.

Sitting meditation was very difficult for Elaine so James didn't further encourage something that would frustrate her. Body boarding in waves Elaine enjoyed and she went out when James went surfing at Makena Shores. They also hiked into some waterfalls, immersing themselves in nature, which contained inherent states of Divinity that can keep humans emotionally balanced, through the negative ions they emit. Their sexual encounters in the feminine energy of Maui seemed to calm Elaine, likewise. The island just seemed to make all things appear and feel better!

Upon their return to Virginia, James and Elaine bought a small farm of over twelve acres, hoping to enable James to learn more about the hidden codes by starting an organic vegetable and fruit farm. He was already an award winning landscape designer and contractor, but James had never run an organic farm. He had certainly studied the concepts and applications of it and had a vegetable garden when he was a boy, but never been responsible for a commercial organic enterprise. James also read an article that indicated there was a study showing certain endorphins were stimulated when a person worked with soil and planting plants and trees and flowers and vegetables. So while James had experienced the mood elevating effects of endorphins while landscaping, he was looking forward to taking a raw piece of land and turning it into a viable organic farm.

The enterprise would involve importing good topsoil and a lot of horse manure so James could terrace a hillside to improve growth and trap rainwater so it would percolate into the soil, as per the concepts of permaculture. He also constructed a greenhouse from high strength plastic fabric to start vegetable seedlings and grow vegetables during the snowy Virginia winters. The more James planted and constructed things, the more excited he became about organic farming. He planted a variety of fruit trees, nut trees and various berry vines and strawberries. Many vegetables and melons and squashes were planted and they grew rapidly in the Virginia spring and summer.

However keeping his vegetables free from the numerous insects in Virginia proved to be a real challenge, as beetles of various types loved to ravage his crops. At first James used organic insecticides such as BT, insecticidal soap, rotenone (a plant bases insecticide from Jicama), and pyrethrin (a natural, potent insecticide), which worked... more or less. But then the budding organic farmer procured a copy of Louise Riott's book, *Carrots Love Tomatoes Too*, and learned how companion planting could mutually protect two different plants from insects and in many cases were also growth enhancing to each other.

Just one example was James taking action to eliminate his problems with Mexican Bean Beetles and Colorado Potato Beetles. By embedding the plants in alternate rows, the beans provided nitrogen to the potatoes. James also read books by Jules Pheiffer and Rudolf Steiner about potentizing or energizing soil with vortex infused "teas" from manure and mineralized supplements.

But before James did any of the alternative planting, he terraced the hillside with timbers and backfilled with topsoil and tilled horse manure, chicken manure, iron sulfate and gypsite (calcium sulfate) into the top soil and the upper areas of the top of the hillside that had native soil; all in preparation to allow his vegetables to grow at astonishing rates.

James also followed myriad concepts foundational in the Findhorn Garden, created by Peter and Eileen Caddy and their associates. Since the garden was known to grow incredibly large and great tasting vegetables, James knew he could not go wrong using their knowledge and practices. And so all of the things James studied allowed him to have a totally organic garden that was productive and tasteful beyond anything he could have imagined. He also used holographic pyramids hanging over some of his crop to stimulate accelerated growth. These pyramids attracted and focused electromagnetic energy/life force/chi/prana into plants just like they did to people... and James certainly had a lot of experience with this!

James then likened the experience of his organic farm with the actual "living of a life" on Earth, and it became clear that with a good foundation and preparation for life—just like a well prepared soil—good fruits could be born in his personal life as well as in organic agriculture. James held a new template of living; he had already surmised that "The Hidden Codes of God" were indispensible templates, or guides, to living life at the highest level possible—far beyond that which almost everyone thought possible. To James, whether there were problems encountered during life's experiences, or in organic agriculture, thorough preparation was the indispensible ingredient, as it were!

James was more than elated with the reaction people gave who bought his produce; consistently amazed and grateful that food could taste so good. It was easy for James, in regard to fruits and vegetables, but to have a tasteful life was more difficult for him, especially when his wife was subject to wide mood swings and had a very violent temper!

James and Elaine subsequently took a second trip to Hawaii: first Oahu and then Maui. This particular trip was the result of rewards points earned on James' credit card. Oahu did not much appeal to either of them, but it did give James a chance to link up with his cousin and family. The most memorable thing about the trip was his cousin's wife constantly trying to over-control the behavior of her adorable and intelligent son, Jonathan. The familiar "control" brought back memories of James' childhood and how his father would try to control his behavior; her parenting behavior was contentious for James, because he truly was a free spirit who had long followed his own path.

Jonathan was much like James was as a boy. James kept telling his mother, June, just how much he liked Jonathan and what a great kid he was! June just ignored James, leaving him to wonder how much of the hidden codes his mother would squelch out of the young boy, trying to control his every move. James remembered the intuitive expression of joy, such as expressed by Jonathan, which is the secret ingredient to happiness in life! James had learned from "The Hidden Codes of God" that this unfettered expression of joy is as close to divinity—God, as anything that anyone can express! James wrestled with his remembrance of Jesus' behest to the crowds to let the children come forward so he could embrace them!

The entire situation bothered James immensely as once again he was forced to recall how his father attempted to suppress his unfettered joy. One time when James was being his goofy, divine self, his father said, "I told you not to be stupid, you moron!"

The situation with Jonathan had to remain as it was; it was time for James and Elaine to go to Maui and they were anticipating it very much because of the strong feminine energy there. Maui really smoothed out Elaine's personality and James was very relaxed likewise and could feel his heart opening even more. It was on Maui, that Elaine and James' son, Rob, would be conceived, although it would not be self-evident at first.

The conception of Rob was especially memorable for two reasons. First, just before James was ready to explode into an orgasm, Elaine told him that she was no longer using her birth control and asked if he still want to continue having sex. Unfortunately for James, he was so enthralled in the energy of sexual delight he proceeded to his impending orgasm. Secondly, it was completed in the light of James not being ready to have children until Elaine detoxified herself from her alcohol and drug addictions, which had not yet occurred. It was just another example of the half-baked decisions Elaine was prone to make.

It was about a month after James and Elaine returned to Virginia they found out Elaine was pregnant. The news really stunned James, as his mind pondered just how irresponsible it was for a prospective mother to conceive without first being clean of alcohol and drugs. It took James several weeks to really deal with the inconsiderate and reckless decisions of his wife. He could not stop thinking how irresponsible Elaine's decisions were, and taking a big chance that her child might not be born normal.

Elaine was most desirous of having a baby girl and planned to call her Tiffany Elaine. However, James told Elaine that the baby would be a boy; he intuited a reality that did not sit well with Elaine and she questioned the veracity of his insight. Elaine got a psychic reading when James and Elaine where they sold crystals, gemstones, jewelry and pyramids during an exhibit at the Heart to Heart Festival in Washington D.C. The psychic told her that the baby would be a girl and Elaine returned to their booth beaming with joy when she told James, "The baby is going to be a girl!"

James just wryly smiled and said, "If that is what you want to believe, Elaine, that is ok with me but, he still is going to be a boy. The psychic was reading your thoughts, which are powerful, and read you instead of the baby."

Elaine had yet another explosive moment, "That is a bunch of crap. This woman has been a psychic for forty years so she knows what she is talking about and that is that!"

"Well that psychic could have one hundred and forty years psychic experience," James retorted, "but she still is reading your own powerful thoughts and not those of the baby. I tell you this not to upset you but to prepare you properly for the baby's birth, without having false expectations."

"Don't want to hear it." Elaine was stalwart. "I don't believe you!"

James was not upset by Elaine's refusal to acknowledge his intuition. It was immensely easier to let her think whatever she wanted so things could be more peaceful. Months later, during an ultrasound at the gynecologist's office, it was revealed that James was in fact correct in his assessment that the child would be a boy as the imaging clearly indicated that there were testicles and a penis. This really knocked Elaine on her ass and completely undid her fantasyland perspective. James just smiled wryly but chose not to gloat about his earlier prediction.

An ultrasound was prompted by the midwife, Trinlie, who was supposed to deliver the baby, but she detected the baby was breach and acknowledged she could not complete the delivery unless she had experienced help to aid her, which she did not have. Not only did the ultrasound reveal the sex of the baby—and that in fact it was breach—it additionally revealed that the umbilical cord was wrapped around the baby's neck at least twice. The status of the umbilical cord was why James was unsuccessful using psycho kinesis to reverse the baby from the breach position. He tried several different nights to no avail, and the ultimate decision was made that the baby, actually a son, would be delivered by Caesarian Section due to the breached position and the umbilical cord around the its neck.

James was in the delivery/operating room for the Caesarian delivery. When they cut into Elaine's womb, he saw blood and fluid squirting in the air. That did not concern him—his only concern was that Elaine and his son were ok and both came through the ordeal without complications. James had no idea how emotional the birth of his son would be for him. He was the first person to really bond with his son, Robert, because Elaine was still under the effect of anesthesia from having her womb sown back together.

The new father was not prepared for the impact this would have on him. He was very tranquil and humbled by the whole birth scenario, but Elaine finally woke up from the effects of the anesthesia, and she felt cheated she was not the first person to bond with her son. James could completely understand her feeling, but was pragmatic enough to know it was not possible under the circumstances of the birth.

Many people congratulated James and Elaine on the birth of Robert and told them how proud they must be. James was humble in his response, "I am not proud, because I had such a small part in this. This is the work of the Creator and not myself or Elaine, even though the ordeal was very difficult on Elaine."

People were rather taken aback from James' response and commented uniformly how unassuming he seemed and how he was different from his casual and humorous self.

Indeed, James was rather astonished by his reaction himself. After the birth, Elaine began showing signs of post partum depression and James needed to step up his role during the baby phase of Robert's life. In fact, James did just this, spending a lot of time holding and hugging his son and quieting him down when he became colicky, which was often.

Young Robert's colic condition could be attributed to Elaine's wide emotional swing, which all babies intuit, feel, and experience. This explained why Elaine was rarely successful calming down her son, but did change how the circumstances frustrated her no end. James' secret weapon was the *Gayatri Mantra*, a Sanskrit prayer/rosary he repeated over and over. When James began reciting, "Om Bhur Bhuvah Svah, Tat Savitur Varenyam, Bhargo Devasaya Dheemahe, Dhiyo Yonah Prochodiat," it always quickly calmed down Robert. The power of the Sanskrit words were well known for thousands of years in India, to have a protecting and calming influence on a person!

The Neokoros, and an officer in the Ancient Hermetic Order of Asclepiads, Dr. Henry Smialek, shared the Gayatri mantra with James. James was introduced to Dr. Smailek by the head of the Asclepiads, the hierophant person who brings religious congregants into the presence of that which is deemed holy… Dr. David DeLorea. From both of these men, James learned more of "The Hidden Codes of God" via the teachings of Asclepius, the greatest Greek healer, which vastly exceeded the works of the more renowned, Hippocrates. Asclepius' initial mode of healing was using herbs from the Mediterranean plant palate. But one day, in an epiphany, it was revealed to Asclepius that he could heal people better and faster utilizing lucid daydreaming.

Eventually James would learn this was putting the patient in the level of alpha and theta consciousness and would have significant implications for James when he wrote his second book, for he would rely on this level of consciousness for the organization of some parts of the book.

Elaine's post partum depression continued and she was often found to be overly cranky or depressed. She began seeing a therapist, which was fine with James because he was open to anything that would bring balance and joy to his wife. But when all of a sudden the therapy was proposed to expand to couples' therapy, James balked—he felt the problems he and Elaine were having in their marriage stemmed from Elaine's personal problems. James also remembered the couples' sessions with Dr. Iaducka, and as proficient as James perceived him to be, things improved only for a short period of time and then reverted back to the same dysfunction. James finally relented, but he knew it would not make a permanent difference in his relationship with Elaine.

When the therapist asked both of them to list the changes they would like each other to make, Elaine had a list of fifty-six things. James had a list of two. The first thing on James' list was no arguing after sex, and the second was each would take responsibility for changing themselves. When the therapist asked James if he could meet all fifty-six of Elaine's complaints, his answer was, "No!" When the therapist pushed further James replied, "Because, even if I perform all fifty-six of those changes, Elaine would have another fifty-six things in no time at all. Instead of dealing with her own problems, she deflects her attention away from herself to me. This is a classic case of the subconscious fixing someone else instead of themselves which is classic co-dependency."

196

Needless to say, this response blew away both the therapist and Elaine. James elaborated even more as he explained, "Each of us should take responsibility for changing ourselves and we should accept each other just as we are!" Elaine and the therapist were speechless with a look of astonishment on their faces.

"Is that you final decision James?" the therapist asked.

"Yes it is!" James said. "I have learned that we create our own reality and that the things we do not like in other people are things that they are mirroring back to us from things we are or used to be. Furthermore, I do not need anyone telling me what my shortcomings are… since I already know what they are and I actively work on my faults. But, as to my wife, she chooses to ignore her demons and rather than concentrating on hers, she continues to focus on mine and that is senseless and disingenuous and keeps her distracted and unfocused on her!"

James' comments were not well taken by the therapist or Elaine but it mattered little to him because he knew that these were subtle teachings and hidden codes he learned in the Sage Experience encounter group.

One thing James admired about his wife was that she was very passionate about the world peace movement, started by Barbara Marx Hubbard, called "Peace Vision." James was equally passionate about it because of his involvement in the Vietnam War, and working in special operations for the CIA even though he was not even acknowledged as a soldier "on the books."

James was involved in a lot of triage work on wounded soldiers, including stuffing their guts back into their

stomachs. He also shot innocent civilians—not on purpose—
—but as collateral damage and not really knowing whom the
"enemy" was or who was friendly. All these images of death
and severe injury made a huge impact on James' psyche and
he often had nightmares about them; later it was rather
dangerous being around him when he was dreaming about
the occurrences.

James also saw himself as a warrior in past lifetimes and
these memories were rather grizzly, likewise. James started to
have a hunch that most of the wars of men were the result of
manipulation to optimize corporate profits. He remembered
a speech by President Eisenhower, a general himself, who in
his farewell address upon leaving office, admonished the
populace to be aware of the military-industrial complex and
their propensity to promote wars. And at the heart of this
complex sat the Illuminati, a cabal believed to exercise power
over the worlds' governments and already held considerable
control, directly or indirectly, over banking, industry and
pharmaceuticals!

In light of all of this, James gave serious consideration
during the late 1980's that it would be a good idea if people
began thinking more about peace than war! In reality, it
would take more than two decades for there to become a
worldwide movement! Unfortunately for James, his wife was
more into world peace than personal peace. The reality was
its toll on his and Elaine's relationship. James really could not
get his wife to see the value of "The Hidden Codes of God"
and yet he was sure if he could succeed in his endeavor,
things would turn around for them as a couple. James came
to the conviction that any president and legislator that voted
to go to war, should be on the front lines with their family

and relatives. And he reckoned that if they did so, they would be most hesitant to declare any war or the resolutions related thereto!

The day came when Elaine confronted James and told him, "Things are not working out for me. I am unhappy and want out of this relationship. Can't you see that things are not working for us?"

James was not slow in his response, noting to Elaine, "That is obvious, but things could really be worked out if you would just soften your stance on this and start studying the things I have learned about the hidden codes and daily perform some type of meditation, including the Tai Chi Standing Meditation. If you did, you would see that there is a perfection that permeates the Universe and when we can embrace this, everything else just becomes insignificant and it starts becoming evident. Usually, you see this a little at first and then it becomes more evident. Additionally, I do not favor breaking up since it can have nothing but negative effects on our son."

Elaine did not understand James' response and returned her rebuttal, "James, you know I am from two broken marriages and yet I survived."

James felt compelled to laugh out loud and then declare to Elaine, "You survived? Just barely! In fact, I would contend that you have so many wounds from this as to account for most of the problems you are dealing with, believe it or not! I also know that you and your sister who committed suicide were dealing with issues related to your grandfather, Pappy. I am sure you were both molested. With your mood swings you are not a "picnic" and if I can put up with you, because I choose to put my son first, you should be able to put up with me!"

Elaine, however, was bound and determined to end the relationship. She was also dismayed by the fact that James did not want to have any more children because she was still dead set on having a daughter. She harbored these feelings, despite the fact she relapsed from her drug rehab program and was still greatly stressed with the symptoms of post partum depression and could barely take care of Robert.

Elaine wanted James to file for divorce, instead of her. James was adamant that if she wanted a divorce she should file for one. James eventually figured out that Elaine did not want to pay the filing fees for a divorce. But since he already had a child, had no desire for a divorce. He remembered his father telling him that he only stuck things out with his mother because he did not want his kids to suffer from a broken family; James was bound and determined to do as his father did. James reckoned that his father took this track because his father's father was so mentally ill as to be MIA as a parent, and did not want his children to experience what he did, which included extreme poverty during the Great Depression. However, Elaine, having come from three family breakups, thought such things were the norm and not abnormal in any sense, while James held the thought, *Just goes to show that if you are used to the bizarre and dysfunctional, you could rationalize anything as normal and possibly never know the difference!*

The impending divorce was inevitable and just a matter of time until it was a legal statistic. When it was granted, James was given liberal visitation rights, but what he really wanted custody of his son because of Elaine's volatility and unpredictability. An attorney counseled him that it would be very unlikely the custody would be taken from a birth mother, even considering the circumstances of Elaine's instability. James thought, however, *Eventually I will get custody of my son and I will bide my time until the right opportunity presents itself! The stable and enlightened upbringing of my son is of utmost importance!*

In the meantime, James busied himself, writing his first book about the hidden codes and how God could literally be experienced in our personal lives. He also came across a similar book, *Pathways to God: Experiencing the Living God in Your Everyday Life*, written by Dr. Robert Newton. At some point James joined forces and efforts with Dr. Newton and they compiled and completed a ground breaking text about higher human spirituality and healing. In spite of all of the turmoil in his life, including the loss of his wife Elaine and the impending dissolution of his marriage, James was strongly focused on writing about "The Hidden Codes of God," although he did not indicate them as such.

The book he co-authored with Dr. Newton included tremendous amounts of information about quartz crystals and gemstones—and about pyramids and magnets—in relation to natural healing and the spiritual expansion of consciousness, which James had long before realized was our main purpose on Earth. The book also included other hidden code material including Sanskrit mantras and Tai Chi, which James was becoming a master in practicing. Basically, the book was about the very things that had made an immeasurable difference in James' life!

Concurrent with this achievement, James had almost completed his courses for a Doctorate in Naturopathic Medicine, also known as Natural Medicine. James came to realize using herbs and homeopathic remedies to heal was also part of "The Hidden Codes of God" as opposed to allopathic medicine that used the synthesized active ingredients from herbs without the buffering compounds. James thus realized that the allopathic drugs of conventional medicine ultimately are not in conformance with the Divine Templates of God or the hidden codes, which accounted for the many side effects related to the use of the drugs.

It was James' feeling that "what God has created let no man put asunder," and this should apply to medicines as much as anything else. From James' perspective and his deeper understanding of the "Hidden Codes of God," the iatrogenesis (side effects or consequences) from the use of pharmaceutical medicines should make such a realization self-evident.

CHAPTER 34

When Elaine took Robert to Saudi Arabia with her new husband, her action served to create a great resentment and anger in James because it would be a year until he would see his son again, and then only for a one month duration. Shortly after James entered that state of anger and resentment, lymphatic cancer (Lymphoma) aggressively manifested in his body. All of his lymph glands were very swollen and he felt pain at all these points. He went to an oncologist to confirm what an iridologist had already diagnosed, and what James already knew. He told James treatment must begin immediately, but James was not interested because of what he learned in his studies to become Naturopathic Doctor.

Not realizing the cause of his cancer was his emotions, James used the protocol in *The Grape Cure*, one of the books he studied in becoming a Doctor of Naturopathy or natural medicine. Although the protocol called for eating nothing but grapes, grape juice and raisins for a continuous week, James did this for only three days and on the third day immense amounts of toxins released from his body.

During the period of his cancer detox, James was renovating a house in Washington D.C. and was so weak from the detox that even slowly moving around required the utmost of effort and it felt like he was more dead than alive. At this time, James decided to ask God to take his life and remove him from the Earth. James begged, "Please, just let me die. I feel so weak and un-alive, what is the point of my continued living on Earth?" James' request from the Creator for death was ignored and he was told, not in a voice, but in thoughts, that he needed to remain on Earth so that he could finish his tasks. These included raising his son and his eventual writing and teaching ventures. Shifting to a different frame of mind, James gutted things out and in a week began to feel immensely better; all signs of Lymphoma had left his body without relying on surgery, chemotherapy or radiation. James had studied the dangers of these oncology protocols and he could see they were all barbaric and even worse, ineffective treatments. He believed although they may show results for a short period of time, eventually, for most people, the cancers always return.

James learned how chemotherapy only makes cancer cells go into hiding, eventually to return to an active state in a patient's body, still alive and quite viable. He also learned radiation only causes the cancer cells to move to another area, and meanwhile, severely damages and compromises anything that is exposed to them. And finally, James learned how surgery only causes cancer to spread; primarily, the purpose of a tumor is to localize toxins and when you remove the "partitioning" function, the cancer can spread very rapidly.

In his studies James came to believe that oncology is basically contrary to the hidden codes and has become yet another way to deceive the populace; to have them believe oncology protocols are the only way to treat cancer. Even more outrageous is the fact that in almost all states, the only legal ways to treat cancer is with oncology protocols. This leaves an ineffective and deceptive monopoly in power and it subverts people's free will and freedom to act as their own judge of how they should heal themselves. If oncology worked so well it would be self evident as to how well this cancer treatment worked and no laws would be necessary to sustain a disingenuous monopoly! The diabolical aspects of this annoyed James but also gave him the passionate resolve to treat patients for cancer without a toxic treatment, which included Aloe Vera Therapy, Hydrogen Peroxide Therapy, the Budwig Protocol of using low fat cottage cheese and raw flax seed oil, essiac tea, the chaparral plant, ultra violet light, near infra red, chelation therapy, an alkalized diet and the Grape Diet, among others.

James then discovered Louise L. Hay's book, *You Can Heal Your Life* and it was like a bible devoted to healing through the removing of the offending and/or corresponding emotions. Actually the concept was found in the wheelhouse of Christian Science and Asclepias, which are within the parameter of "The Hidden Codes of God." "Wow!" James thought, "The more I learn the more the hidden codes are revealed… the more the codes are revealed, the more I learn. But I am sure that I will learn even more about these codes; I feel it intuitively. But this romantic relationship stuff is harder to master. Obviously, I screwed up divorcing Ann. That really bit me in the butt because her heart was open and she could deal with her baggage and she really loved me and I really loved her! Through all the relationships I have had since I left her, I have uncovered so many things related to 'The Hidden Codes of God' but my romantic relationships have held so much dysfunction."

There is an obvious synchronicity here for me regarding relationships. James thought. *It is undeniable when the same thing or similar things keep coming up many times! There must be some things hidden in my subconscious that manifest this drama in my life! I know*

Robert J. Newton, J.D., N.D

for a fact I have created all this, just as I learned in "The Sage Experience" encounter group, and from my subsequent study of quantum mechanics!"

CHAPTER 35

Sadly, James was faced with selling the organic farm he
had built from scratch because Elaine would not allow
him to assume her half of the loan and the property
would be most difficult for him to refinance, considering his
shaky financial situation. James wanted to keep the farm and
his new girlfriend, Viviana, urged him to do so. James first
met Viviana at "The Soul Connection," a kind of a New Age
show, where he had an exhibit in Washington D.C. The
crystals entranced her, as did the other minerals and jewelry
made from the gemstones. Apparently, she was quite taken
with James, as well, but he noticed this less because he was
concentrating on another woman who he already knew and
was attracted to. Viviana talked some to James at the show
and found out he was quite angry with his ex-wife, Elaine, for
taking his son to Saudi Arabia. Viviana mentioned that she
had become certified in a protocol that allowed people to
remove their negative emotions almost immediately.

Anyway, a couple days after the show, Viviana, who took
one of James' *Harmonic Environments* business cards after
buying several quartz and tourmaline crystals, called him and
invited him over to the house where she lived, offering to
remove his angry emotions regarding his ex-wife. When
James arrived she hugged him intensely and then took him by
the hand and said, "Let's go outside by the lake where things
are calm and relaxing." So with Viviana, hand in hand, James
went outside and they sat on a bench near the lake in the

shade, which gave them shelter from the hot summer sun in Virginia. They sat down and almost immediately Viviana began squeezing James' hand and in no time at all had progressed to kissing him. This really excited James, as he had not kissed a woman for many months, because of things going downhill with Elaine.

Pretty soon, James and Viviana had their arms around each other and they were in a strong embrace; the passion between them increased and their lips locked for long periods of time as their tongues touched and flitted about each other's mouth. Viviana could detect that James' penis was becoming very hard while she probed his crotch with her hand. Finally she said, "In your condition James, it is obvious we need to visit my bedroom." And James just nodded, "Yes" as Viviana took him by the hand and led him up the stairs to her bedroom.

As soon as the duo entered the bedroom, they both began to take off each other's clothes and James then pulled Viviana down with him onto her bed. That is when things got intense because they were more relaxed and could really hug and caress and kiss each other with reckless abandon. James ravaged Viviana's breasts, kissing them and then lightly biting them, which just turned Viviana on even more; she squeezed James tightly with her arms around him as she felt wave after more intense wave of the energy of love flow into her heart.

The more turned on James found Viviana became, the more excited he became and was soon overcome with the energy of love entering into his heart. This foreplay continued for about an hour because the energy between James and Viviana just kept building.

Finally, James moved his head down to Viviana's vagina and began kissing her inner thighs with many kisses, moving about from place to place. This made her quiver and squirm in delight and she yelled at James, "Stop teasing me! You are driving me crazy."

"Your energy is driving me crazy likewise," James replied. Finally James put his tongue into Viviana's vagina and began thrusting it deeply into her and then flitted back and forth. But when James started concentrating on her clitoris, Viviana was overcome with the feelings of love and the euphoria that accompanied the other feelings and emotions. Then Viviana told James, "Please switch around so that I can take care of your penis while you are taking care of my clitoris."

James replied, "I would but if I did I would explode in your mouth. It is taking all of my concentration and tightening of my anal sphincter muscles to prevent my orgasm. Let me concentrate on you because it is extremely enjoyable for me to see you so blissed out!"

So James kept working away and could tell that Viviana was close to exploding into an orgasm. The anticipation of this excited him as much as it affected Viviana! As she erupted into some incredible moaning and thrusting her hips, James knew that she had reached the more extreme realms of love akin to heaven. So in no time at all, James penetrated Viviana's vagina with his penis and thrust into, her slowly at first, because he wanted Viviana to have a simultaneous orgasm with him. As James kissed Viviana's lips, fondled her breasts, and thrust again and again into her vagina, he sensed the corresponding thrusting of Viviana's hips and knew she was close to her second climax. As he sensed her deepening emotions, James loosened his anal sphincter muscles so that his sperm could be released into Viviana's vagina.

In no time at all, they were pounding into each other and both screamed out loud as they climaxed together. Viviana's fingernails dug into James back and she writhed with delight. Both of them had so much energy streaming into their hearts and heads that the intenseness caused their screams. When finished, they both completely relaxed and melted into each other's arms. Being in this relaxed state allowed both of them to circle the energy of love not only in their own bodies but back and forth to each other's hearts. James languished in what was akin to a perpetual motion machine... in the energy that flowed between them without effort.

Literally, they had attracted the life force, chi, prana, atomic force of the Creator into a greater manifestation than either of them had ever experienced before. It was many months since James had sex and several years for Viviana so they were both highly primed and ready to experience the bliss of an intense energy of sexual union. James was grateful Viviana took the initiative to seduce him! They were in the tight embrace of each other for many hours and really didn't sleep much that night. James considered, *who could sleep anyway when ensconced in an energy force field of love?*

CHAPTER 36

Once again James was confronted with the power of the underlying aspects of the energy of love, represented by various traditions that had that contained and explained the hidden codes as was Viviana. She became as enthralled with James as he was with her. In the heat of the passion of sexual conjoining, James saw the most compelling light and essence radiating from around the face of Viviana. She was attractive and shapely already, but this energy factor that James perceived as literally being drawn to a higher dimension, revealed things normally unseen!

These things were discussed and portrayed in *Sexual Secrets,* by Slinger and Douglas and in Taoist texts; James was so glad that he had studied these books. Much of the information James had brought through from his previous incarnations on Earth, but it was gratifying to have the confirmation of things always sensed regarding sexuality.

In the subsequent times James and Viviana joined sexually, they experienced a recurring mind-blowing consciousness of expanded energy that was profound and compelling. Viviana didn't carry the baggage of destructive behavior prevalent in Elaine, making easy and pleasant to be with her. James was able to focus on circulating the life force of the Creator and be in a natural state of wonderment and bliss. But there was a not-so-mundane issue that faced James—his inability to refinance the farm mortgage so that he could remain living on the farm and reap the benefits of his hard and dedicated work to develop it. James sought financial aid from his ex-girlfriend, Annette, and he thought she would be interested since he remembered she had received a lot of money from the sale of a business; unfortunately, Annette did not want to make this type of commitment. Most likely, it was because James was not firm in his original romantic commitment to her. He could easily understand this!

Viviana wanted James to continue living in Virginia even after he sold the farm. But James had an astrolocality astrologer complete a chart of the most optimum places for him to live. The chart basically showed where James currently lived in Virginia was not optimum for him but where he lived previously in California was highly ideal. Additionally, James knew he had made karmic mistakes in his divorce from Ann, his wife of sixteen years. Simply put, she really did nothing to even remotely warrant James divorcing her. She was always loyal to him and faithful to wit. She was an incredible lover and knew more about "The Hidden Codes of God" than anyone with whom James had been involved romantically. The fact that she decided to withdraw from the Tibetan Foundation not only was not a valid reason to divorce someone. It would not have been the right move for anyone with a detached perspective, which James obviously did not have during the events surrounding their divorce.

So James sold the farm, said his goodbyes to the amazing Viviana and began moving his things back to California. He explained to Viviana that he considered her quite an incredible person and that she was nothing but wonderful, but that it was imperative for him to right the wrongs he had wrought against Ann. Viviana understood and admired James for his perspectives, but to say that she was not hurt by his actions would have been more than an understatement. James knew that he not only was remiss in not keeping his marriage vows to Ann, but his actions had negatively affected her financially. Even though he gave her more than half of the marital estate in the divorce, the stress from dealing with economic problems had over time affected Ann's health.

James had learned so much and met so many incredible people during his stay in Virginia, although financially things were always tenuous and there was always the stress of having enough money to cover his bills. The organic farm was something James was going to miss immensely, even though there was a lot of hard work involved. He was grateful for his involvement in The Heart to Heart Festival in Washington D.C. and the contacts he had made there. He was also had fond remembrances of the New Age expo at Johns Hopkins University and the Psi Symposium in Charlottesville, Virginia. He remained in contact with some of the people he met there including James Raughton, his first publisher. He learned so much from the Ancient Hermetic Order of Asclepiads, especially Dr. David DeLorea and Dr. Henry Smialek, because so many aspects of "The Hidden Codes of God" were revealed to him and he chose to become a third level Asclepiad.

James was additionally thankful he could teach classes on crystal and gemstone energy and pyramid dynamics and magnetic acupuncture at various festivals and symposiums and metaphysical and New Age bookstores. Writing *Pathways to God: Experiencing the Living God in Your Everyday Life* pleased James, as did the wide-ranging information contained therein. Truly, it was a distillation of things he had accumulated from the hidden codes and what he taught in his classes. James also was able to earn his Doctorate in Naturopathic Medicine; over time adding to myriad things learned about "The Hidden Codes of God" that would serve him well in his experiences in California.

CHAPTER 37

The first thing James did when he got back to California was to go and see Ann. He had talked to her on the phone and apprised her that he was selling his farm and returning to California and wanted to come by and see her. He had actually seen her once in the intervening years when he was visiting his parents in California with his two-year-old son, Robert. And so they talked and enjoyed each other's company and marveled at the mischief that Robert could create and how he could finger paint with his food, rather than eating very much of it.

When James went to Ann' house, which formerly was his own home, he was as glad to see Ann she was him. James commented how unhappy he was about the tree trimmers that had butchered the trees he had planted two decades previously. Ann responded, "You are right and it hurt me immensely also to see your work so defiled. The tree trimmer promised to be here when his workers were doing the work and he wasn't. Such magnificent presences should not be treated in such a manner. Can you fix the trees, James? For sure I would have had you do the work if you were here because no one understands trees like you!"

"Yes I can," James replied, "but it will take several years to pull it off since it must be done in stages as the tree responds. I appreciate your acknowledging my abilities."

So James suggested that they go to Rutabagorz Restaurant where they served health food; a place they had enjoyed many times previously. And as they talked, and waited for their food, James could see a look in Ann's eyes that let him know she still really liked him; Ann detected the same in James by his body language. So there was nothing uncomfortable between them even though five years had passed since they had done anything together. Ann asked James where he was going to live and he said he wanted to live close to the beach so he could surf very often, something he could not do in Virginia since he lived three and a half hours from the closest beach and waves. But right now he was not thinking about waves, but rather Ann.

James began to say something and it was hard to get it out but finally he said, "You know Ann, what I did to you when I divorced you it was wrong and I ask for your forgiveness. I was getting bad advice about our previous relationship and it led me to make some very bad decisions. But in the end, bad advice or not, I am responsible for making my own decisions. I apologize for any hardship for which you may have endured because of my actions. We were a team and I took vows to for us to be together, for better or worse. I did not honor my end of the bargain and for that I am ashamed. And I regret any hardship I may have inflicted upon you. I have learned many things about "The Hidden Codes of God" that we were uncovering and that part of my life has been rewarding. The romantic relationship thing has had its ups and downs, but mostly down. Do you remember when I left for Virginia I told you, who knows, we might even get back together some day?"

"Yes I do," Ann responded, "and I am glad you are back. That Tibetan Foundation was a real relationship breaker... look at how many couple's relationships crashed and burned there! But what about your girlfriend in Virginia, how does she factor into things?"

"Well," James replied, "she was really nice but it became self evident to me that I needed to come back here and right things, if you are amenable to that. She was less than happy about my decision but she understood when I explained everything. It was tough, but I realized I needed to deal with the bad karma I created with you and really the only way to do that is to do what you need to make things right. Certainly, I never bought that lame ass idea that if you confessed your sins they would just be forgiven. That literally violates one of the laws of physics that says, "For every action, there is an equal and opposite reaction." Looked at objectively, the invalidity of this forgiveness via the confession of your sins doctrine is starkly apparent—at least to us geniuses!" James laughed out loud.

"Yes," Ann said, "you are correct and I feel so good you have recognized that. However, I hold absolutely no animosity toward you, although your actions hurt me a lot emotionally. But the fact that you have grown and made the realizations you have shared with me is really special. I really did not know you wanted to get back together with me but I would like that."

"You know," James exclaimed, "we were really good together in many ways. After what I have been through, this became blaringly true kind of like I got violently kicked in the head! Actually, I made this realization soon after I became married to Elaine. Wow, what a wakeup call—a loud wakeup call to wit!"

"I will get an apartment in Huntington Beach, close to the ocean and we can date during the week," James explained.

"And then you can stay here on the weekend and we can spend more time together, if you are amenable to that, James," Ann said.

"Yeah, that would be real nice, like the old days." James replied. So James found and rented an apartment about a mile from the beach and a couple of blocks from a health food store. He retrieved some of his old landscaping customers and added some new ones in short order, due to referrals and advertising. And he also began treating patients in his natural medicine practice.

But James was more excited about being able to surf four or five days a week because it was something that took him to a deeper level of consciousness and thus put him in a state of a deeper interface/connection with the Creator. When James got inside the tube of a wave he was most certainly in a higher dimension of being and consciousness. These things were very addictive, but more akin to a good addiction; something beneficial that was relaxing and euphoric! James felt sorry for people who never had this experience with the ocean because it was just so magical, yet hard to completely describe unless you had actually surfed yourself. It definitely left James exhilarated. A lot of creative inspiration came very easily to James after he surfed which he applied to landscape designs.

One day when James and Ann were eating at a restaurant she said to him, "I saw this advertisement in "Yoga Journal" about a class in Kundalini Yoga. I would like to go to that and think you would like it too."

"Well," James replied, "I already know most things about Kundalini, having had intense energy awakenings multiple times, and also I am a Tai Chi master so I don't see the need."

"But," Ann protested, "Do you think you know everything about this—really?"

"I guess I really should keep an open mind on this and since I know you want to go and will not drive there yourself, I guess we should take the weekend class," James replied.

CHAPTER 38

When James and Ann arrived for the first level Kriya Kundalini Yoga class in Marina del Ray, they entered the room and saw Yogi Marshall Govindan, their teacher. James looked into Govindan's eyes and could tell he was intense and yet serene, which gave James confidence that Govindan would be competent teacher of Kriya Yoga, an ancient system of protocols/practices the increase of one's energy and enhance their levels of conscious. When Govindan talked about his past spiritual and work experiences, James and Ann were even more convinced they had a teacher also experienced in "life and living."

The class consisted of Asanas, which were stretching and counter-poses, Kriya Dhyana meditations, and Kriya Kundalini Pranayam, which is not exactly, but essentially, a very extended breathing meditation. Half of each of these three things was taught on each day. So first, the group completed half of the Asanas; James and Ann found them very functional and useful in stretching the muscles and adjusting the spinal column. Next, Govindan taught the first half of the Kriya Dhyana meditations and they practiced it for about fifteen minutes, but James did not think it was such a big deal.

But when Govindan taught them the first Pranayam breathing element and James practiced it, he was actually quite amazed when he began having a Kundalini energy awakening, which was quite akin to having an intense electromagnetic energy coursing throughout his body! His face felt as if it was on fire and his breathing and heart also stopped and found he was barely able to relate to the third dimension. Govindan noticed James experience and asked him, "Were you in Samadhi?"

James replied, "Yes I was," even though he did not know technically what Samadhi really was. But he assumed, and rightly so, that it was part of the Kundalini experience.

After this experience, James knew he and Ann had found many things that could be considered "The Hidden Codes of God." Kriya Kundalini Yoga and especially Pranayam provided techniques to vastly altered states of consciousness. The immense value of this did not escape James or even Ann. Neither realized it at the time, but it would be only the first of many amazing things they would learn from Govindan. James further realized he had actually been doing the Pranayam breathing for over a decade before he was officially taught such. And from this James further recognized he must have done Pranayam in at least one other lifetime and most likely many more, because this breath was very easy for him, but difficult for the rest of the class!

So the rest of the weekend was full of things that would be very useful in the lives of James and Ann and they made several new friends from this class!

CHAPTER 39

The first night James and Ann spent together at her house caused a lot of energy, revealed by electricity in the air. Each knew this was occurring because the life force/prana/chi in their bodies mingled together without them even touching… and a much stronger energy field was created from the combination than when segregated into their individual bodies. This is a common phenomenon that occurs when a romantic couple with a longstanding history and who have not been dulled by the familiarity of their relationship come into close proximity to each other.

Regardless, there was a magical feeling in the air neither James nor Ann could ignore! Possibly the roses that James brought Ann enhanced the energy; there is information in "The Hidden Codes of God" about the highly evolved energy and essence of flowers—especially roses. Actually, some of the most poignant information about this topic was unpublished and brought through by James from the Akashic records, which is all the information of the Universe which is saved for posterity and made accessible to people with highly developed intuition. This occurred when James did a public channeling session for the Tibetan Foundation, just after James and Ann were divorced. The information was related to how highly evolved the plant kingdom is in general and how more evolved are flowers and flowering plants and trees, including plants and trees that bare fruits and plants that bare vegetables. The rose was given the highest evolution due to it stunning flowers, many of which are fragrant and have the qualities of very intense aromatherapy!

So most likely, in light of all of this, the roses were promulgating the intense energetic atmosphere… as if they were even really needed because Ann's "Opium" perfume was highly intoxicating to James. When James took Ann's hand, sparks began to fly and when he put his arms around her waist and hers around his, there was an instant melding of their energies and everything felt nothing but right. Both James and Ann savored the embrace, soaking it in without even trying to kiss each other, which allowed the energies around them to be significantly augmented!

A higher energy shift occurred when James and Ann finally began kissing, at first softly with many small pecks and then with increasing intensity and lengthier kisses, including rubbing their tongues together. James was so high and elated from the intensity he told Ann, "I must have been an idiot to ever leave what we created. The subconscious mind/mortal mind/brain-computer can really mess with your head and lead you to make really bad decisions."

Ann's exclamation was rather intense, "I really do not care about the past right now so let's just move forward! At least that is my intention; I am going to get into something more comfortable and invite you to consider meeting me in the bedroom!"

James had no problem doing just that and he removed all of his clothes and underwear and lay down on Ann's bed. Shortly thereafter, Ann entered the bedroom from the bathroom in very sexy lingerie. By this time his penis was extremely engorged with blood and energized to the max. But

James knew that focusing on the exhilarating sensations in his penis should not let him forget about circulating that energy into his head, especially at the crown (the top) and the medulla oblongata (back of the head). By doing this, he would be pulled into higher realms/dimensions whereby any orgasm is intensely magnified.

It is this energy by which the man needs to ignite the woman since she is a negative or receptive polarity and receives energy; the man is the positive or igniting and energizing polarity as the attractor and dispenser of it. This is the essence of which God is comprised, dispensed through an atomic field. James had learned this from the hidden codes; he also learned when both sexual partners are aware of these truths, everything then moves to a higher realm or dimension. It is true this happens to some degree in most sexual liaisons, whether there is a conscious awareness of it or not. But with both James and Ann being cognizant, the effect was greatly magnified; being conscious of these energy characteristics allows the partners to direct it to each other The couple can then share the greater energy presence, are more attracted to each other, and access more of the Universal life force!

That is just what occurred as Ann lay on the bed; James first softly and then furiously kissed her, likened to a decrescendo and a crescendo. This allowed them to experience the energy in succeeding, intensely magnifying waves. The result of each higher level of energy created was the actual dematerialization of the body into to its tangible Spirit, energy actuality. This was something that was often alluded to by Mary Baker Eddy, who was a dispenser of parts of "The Hidden Codes of God' through *Science and Health with*

Key to the Scriptures. However, Mrs. Eddy never talked about sexuality. In fact, she said that all sensuality should be avoided. And yet Indian tantric sex books say this degree of sensuality can take couples to the highest realms of spiritual bliss. James and Ann chose to combine these two disciplines taken from "The Hidden Codes of God" into something more meaningful than the two concepts considered separately.

All of this energy and sensuality was growing as James and Ann embraced each other on the bed. The electricity coming from their hands and heads was so intense that they energized each other through their sharing. Although the energy was intense, it caused an extreme relaxation in their bodies and it was this relaxed state that allowed the magnitude of the energy to be fully experienced. It put them in a deep theta brainwave trance, but what was going on transcended brainwave and resided in the realm of God consciousness. James saw a distinct glow around Ann's face and drew on his experience with Kirilian photography that explored certain photographic techniques used to capture the phenomenon of electrical coronal discharges. It gave him the frame of reference to know this was more than an illusion and actually a real manifestation of light. James shared with her, "You know, Ann, your whole face is lighted up. You are so beautiful. It certainly seems surreal but I know it is not an illusion."

In a whispered voice Ann replied, "I guess that is why you appear so sexy yourself because your face is beaming light likewise. And, like you, I know what I am seeing is not an illusion!"

By now, James could have consummated the deal with Ann, but being the Divine Energy junkie he had become, it was not going to occur for quite a while because James was too busy kissing Ann's entire body. The experience was like being smothered in kisses but it was the kind of smothering someone would want if they had opened their entire heart and open to moving with whatever delight manifested itself. Ann sensuously stroked James' neck and spine and kissing and biting his neck and it only turned James on even more.

James concentrated on kissing Ann's inner thighs, which prompted her vaginal juices to flow, and when James began pleasuring her vagina, strong vaginal odors stimulated him even more. Ann was so aroused that it was a very short time before she had an orgasm, after which James said to her, "Let's do the sitting sexual position because I feel so much closer to you that way."

"I like that sense of intimacy also," Ann responded. So as James entered Ann, he was close to exploding, but he contracted his sphincter muscles and delayed his ejaculation.

Tightly bonded to each other in a passionate embrace, the extreme intimacy of the moment was not lost on either James or Ann. It allowed them to lose themselves in each other, so that as they both began a simultaneous orgasm, the energy released put them in the deepest theta trances and their awareness of everything was enhanced. James then thought, *Surely this is a manifestation of the seventh name of God from the Kabbalistic "72 Names of God" which says, "Aleph Kaf Aleph," restoring things to their perfect state.* At this time, it would have been impossible to conceive a more perfect state of consciousness that anyone could experience.

After their orgasms, energy releases and the coupling thereof, in this close to perfect state, James and Ann held to this heightened bliss for many hours. In an extended state of theta consciousness and trance, they both began to see subtle aspects of "The Hidden Codes of God," which they had never considered before. Such was the effect of the realm of intuition and Divine Mind and Divine Intelligence they both entered. The experience rather forcefully reinforced the contention held by both James and Ann that sex was far more than "just fun with friction." Additionally, they were both sure the prana, chi, or life force content in their bodies had been vastly raised by the assiduous practice of Kriya Kundalini Pranayam and it had translated into their elevated sex-capade. Neither had an explanation for the higher levels of energy and consciousness experienced in their sexual union! Certainly it did not come from watching porn movies!

James and Ann had been studying Tantric and Taoist sexual techniques, whereby the male was to withhold or suppress ejaculation. The purpose was to keep the intense prana or life force energies circulating for a longer period of time. James had tried the technique several times and found he didn't get as much blast from the energies flowing into the spine and head as when he ejaculated. And he found that his ejaculation did not suppress his ability to keep the intense pranic energies circulating within himself and Ann. In the afterglow of their orgasms, the pair found the intense energies continued to circulate for many hours!

CHAPTER 40

Infused with greater creativity in his landscaping business, James searched for new healing protocols as a result of his Kriya Kundalini Yoga practices, especially practice of Pranayam breathing. The more of the breaths James infused into his body, the more energized and curious he became. The first protocol James studied and became certified in was Sound Signature Healing, taught by its founder Sharry Edwards. While he had trouble relating to Sharry, James definitely saw the benefit of the protocols and was intrigued by using sound frequencies to promote healing, and thus balances a person to a more optimum state of consciousness.

James was familiar with the effectiveness of toning, a type of non-vocal singing, and Tibetan bowls and bells and tuning forks to energize chakra points (energy centers in the body) to deal with the emotional causes of disease. And James was further familiar with the sound cubicles at the Temple of Saqqara in Egypt and the frequencies that have emanated from them many thousands of years since the cubicles were created. And James had heard the deep throat toning of The Gyume Tibetan monks and even performed some himself, but knew Sound Signature most related to the Tibetan monk deep throat toning.

Sound Signature uses tones from the diatonic scale at a subwoofer level; the tones are very low. In order to ascertain which tones should be directed to a patient, their voice patterns from talking had to be analyzed, using a chromatic tuner and denoting which notes were indicated. And in all cases a patient has at least one tone that is not present in the spectral analysis of their voice tones; this provides the missing tone—at the subwoofer level in the diatonic scale—and usually brings relief and/or healing conditions in the body.

Toning is a powerful healing modality as well as an area and realm of "The Hidden Codes of God." But there was so much more for James to learn, such as knowledge about magnetic healing from Dr. Jesse Partridge. James had already learned magnetic acupuncture from Dr. Jack Prince's book, *Heal Yourself,* and from Roy Burdett, who taught Dr. Prince. Dr. Partridge used much larger magnets to stimulate acupuncture points than James had previously used. Jesse's approach involved large and powerful magnets placed under the soles of the feet to stimulate all the reflexology points in the feet. These reflexology points are basically the same as acupuncture points except all parts of the body can be accessed from points on the souls of the feet. Dr. Partridge placed a large magnet on the thymus gland to stimulate the immune system with the intent to counteract diseases such as cancer, AIDS, Hepatitis and renal failure.

James was intrigued by this new approach to magnetic healing and the use of magnets on the eyebrows to counteract glaucoma and utilizing them to stimulate the pituitary and pineal glands. Dr. Partridge even talked about a surgeon who had a magnet embedded into the top of his head to continually stimulate the pineal gland, which is the small endocrine gland in the vertebrate brain that produces melatonin. The surgeon had the insertion, hopefully to expand his lifespan. James likewise thought about extended life spans, but the lengthened lifespan he considered was more about the immortality of the human body—for all eternity—as talked about in Kriya Kundalini Yoga and demonstrated by the Yoga Siddhas: Babaji Nagaraj, Agastyar, Boganathur, Valmiki, Kokanavar, Rama Devar and Thirumoolar, among others.

Regardless, James felt he had learned more about the hidden codes than he had previously. The essential thing about using the magnets is that polarity is a crucial factor with some treatments. Some worked better with a negative polarity and others worked better with the other side… positive polarity. Basically, the negative polarity reduces and eliminates pain and infection, whereas the positive polarity energizes things and often loosens knotted muscles and accelerates the regrowth of bone… as long as there is no infection related to the site of treatment.

Basically, James could see that magnetic healing was involved in some way, shape and form with prana, chi, life force—and the electromagnetic properties that emanated there from. Essentially, James found these energies were related to light and fire or atomic photons, which are particles of light. When James composed the second book with Dr. Newton, *A Map to Healing and Your Essential Divinity Through Theta Consciousness,* he learned even more about how magnetic healing functioned.

But, for James, the recognition that magnets often effectuated amazing healing results was enough to know for now. Unfortunately, the healings people experienced with cancer, AIDS, spinal meningitis, hepatitis, Lyme disease, and relief from spinal and joint problems made James and his teachers targets of the FDA and AMA and the FTC; they came to rely on the umbrella of churches to continue practicing their magnetic healing protocols.

The irony of being harassed for being able to heal people quickly, cheaply, and completely, was not lost on James who thought, Wow! *This is just another example of the monopolistic structures created on this planet by the Illuminati. When you threaten their obscene profits, they are quick to attack those people and organizations that would cut into their 'margins.' This is so diabolical; not only are people being overcharged by the powers that be, they are being filled with poisons and not even completely healed—ever!*

James also thought, *each harassment scenario is the result of being able to heal very many things… affordably and completely, as opposed to just treating symptoms with allopathic drugs, which always have side effects. How long will it take before people finally realize the gross fraud involved with all of this? More than one hundred and fifty years ago, Mary Baker Eddy revealed to us how to heal ourselves by claiming the perfectly created heritage that has been given to us by The Creator.*

Concurrently with myriad thoughts that drove his passion, James invested his time studying monthly papers released by "The Journal of Sympathetic Vibratory Physics," edited and sometimes written by Dale Pond. James learned musician, John Keely, used the vibrations of the diatonic musical scales to power perpetual motion machines. Many mathematical formulas were proposed as to how this could be accomplished, but no one seemed to be able to replicate Keely's work to produce their own perpetual motion machines. What James understood was there was a literal similarity between Keely's work and that of Sharry Edwards and "Sound Signature Healing" that indicated the power of sound and vibration and the phonons to effect a change in

232

something—whether to create a perfectly functioning body or an optimally running machine that can generate power without a source of fuel. The materials indicated another aspect of atoms, which were related and complementary to phonons. Once again, as James composed *A Map to Healing and Your Essential Divinity*... he further understood the underlying implications regarding all he learned.

James also experimented with diatonic tuning forks as per the *Cosmic Octave,* by Hans Couseau. He was able to replicate Couseau's work with the tuning forks and how they activated and balanced the chakra energy points in the body. This technique allowed perfect balance within the chakras, the vortexial energy centers in the body that store prana/chi/life force, and distribute them throughout the body to keep it alive and functioning. Also, the vibrations from these tuning forks result in the removing of negative emotions: fear, anger, resentment, irritation and depression, which is effectuated with the release of stored emotions by the sounds they produce.

James was amazed how the method more rapidly helps patients in many situations, where other modalities are slow to provide change. Again, he reckoned his foray into the realm of phonons was also further information of "The Hidden Codes of God." Certainly, it is known to a very few people and thus hidden... and as such, revelatory and expanding the very boundaries of human consciousness and knowledge.

Additionally, James made a magnetic bed on a frame of plywood, covered with a copper screen, and a diamond lattice of steel wire on top of it. Attached to the wire lattice and grid work were negative polarity magnets and quartz and tourmaline crystals, which affected his goal to achieve extreme relaxation in the human body. And in this relaxed state, as per the concepts of Tai Chi, significant amounts of increased energy would course into the body, sometimes creating a healing situation.

Other times patients were to astral project out of their bodies, and still other times... they would have a Kundalini awakening, wherein they were transported forcefully into other dimensions while being infused with so much prana/energy it felt as though their faces were on fire. For some people, it was a break through life experience, but for others... too radically intense.

On this magnetic bed, James used multiple layers of fabric to create a higher energy field according to the work of Wilhelm Reich, and the predestined effect of using dissimilar materials. James' layers included wool, cotton, rayon and silk. The interaction of these dissimilar materials created more life force energy and proved the validity of Reich's contention that combining dissimilar materials would create a higher aggregate energy field than the aggregated energy of the materials measured separately and kept apart from each other.

The concept was easily verified by using dowsing rods to measure the accumulated energy fields! When James placed a ten-foot holographic pyramid made from brass and coated with silver and gold over top of the bed, the energy potential of the magnetic bed was enhanced even more. This was never used for patients who were experiencing the magnetic bed for their first time; only for subsequent usage because of the intensity involved. James knew that an acclimation period was necessary before the pyramid was introduced as a higher energy factor.

A wider purview of "The Hidden Codes of God" was accumulating in James' consciousness and the more he learned, the more new aspects of the hidden codes were revealed to him. In a manner of speaking, James had created his own perpetual motion machine of ideas. As he worked on *A Map to Healing and Your Essential Divinity...* James began to understand how it occurred, but for the time being, the occurrence of this phenomenon was miraculous in and of itself!

Even more things were coming for James and even Ann. Actually it was Ann's idea that they attend a Reiki seminar and James considered it a useful pursuit. When they began the one-day experience with their teacher, Patricia, who was a Master Reiki Healer, the couple could tell she fully comprehended Reiki and how to apply it for healing. Although it was not explained that Reiki concentrated and focused life force energies, James and Ann realized it was the same as prana or chi, and did not have to contemplate the power of employing its practice in a directed manner for healing. Through combining a motion with a short phrase, and then accumulating life force in their hands, James and Ann effected healing on other students in the class. One of the students commented on how unusually powerful the energy was that emanated from James' hands.

Possibly... actually more likely, James was born with this attribute and brought it from a previous incarnation on Earth and forward into this life. But, undoubtedly, James engaging in assiduous amounts of the Tai Chi Standing Meditation and Kriya Kundalini Pranayam was responsible for his enhanced healing energy level, as were previous life developed abilities, which ultimately became even more pronounced in this lifetime. Regardless, the Reiki protocol was similar in many ways to the etheric energy protocols he learned in the Tibetan Foundation more than a decade previously. Both of these disciplines were effective and reliable protocols for healing physical and emotional situations.

Another special healing protocol James learned was "Theta Healing," as conceived by Vianna Stibal. Brett, one of her certified teachers, taught James' weekend class. James saw so much similarity between this practice and Christian Science healing treatments that he knew there must be some great insights into "The Hidden Codes of God." Basically, the protocol was to shift consciousness to theta brainwave and then go through a specific protocol to remove sickness and negative emotions from the body or consciousness, in order to reprogram perfect health and emotional balance.

The problem James saw with the method was that the class was never taught how to get to, or remain in, the state of theta consciousness; he felt it was a rather glaring omission. Unfortunately, the teacher also derided Christian Science practitioners and healers, which immensely offended James.

James asked Brett, "Oh, come on now, do you really have any realistic understanding about Christian Science practitioners?"

The teacher responded, "Actually I do since my mother is friends with a practitioner and she has all these ridiculous idiosyncrasies and rituals and only works within a certain set of hours."

"Your ignorance on these issues is rather glaringly stunning," James exclaimed. "I know at least seven Christian

Science practitioners and none of them act as you claim. Additionally, both my wife and I have called Christian Science practitioners at two and three in the morning and they have always responded. So you really should not speak from a point of ignorance and make gross generalizations about an entire class of things. What you should be concentrating on is giving the class valuable keys to shifting into theta consciousness, rather than ostracizing Christian Science practitioners."

The teacher retorted, "Well, I told the entire class that you know you are in theta when your eyes turn naturally upward and/or flutter. Did you not get that James?"

"Like, duh," James sarcastically replied, "I know all of that. But you have not given practices or protocols for actually getting to the state of upward turned eyes and eyes fluttering. I find this to be a huge omission on your part, and completely stunning and unbelievable. I know at least five reliable ways to get to theta."

"You are making a mountain out of a mole hill," Brett replied.

"And you are putting the cart in front of the horse, Brett," James said. "It is not a problem for me but it sure is for the rest of the class. We have all been remarking about this shift and wondering when you are going to address it. It would appear that your priority of disrespecting Christian Science practitioners should be replaced with explaining theta consciousness."

Nothing significant was resolved by the confrontation with Brett, but James gained the respect of the rest of the class and actually taught many of them his theta enhancing techniques, including the Tai Chi Standing Meditation. Overall, James was successful with the Theta Healing protocols, but resolved he would create an even more comprehensive and reliable method of healing using Theta Healing as a baseline and then enhance and enlarge it. Eventually, James would create the system of Theta Consciousness Healing and Reprogramming.

Both James and Ann were on an upward spiral… learning more and becoming more infused with the hidden codes. Their success came from being focused and having inquisitive, searching minds and a disciplined practice of Tai Chi, Kriya Yoga and the repetition of Sanskrit mantras— similar somewhat to a Rosary, but in the sacred language of Sanskrit. The more of these practices they performed, the more they understood; their consciousness was entrained at a theta level and each realized from their studies that these practices allowed access to the province of the Divine and were a portal thereto.

Mary Baker Eddy, in *Science and Health with Key to the Scriptures*, called this Divine Mind, although she never mentioned theta consciousness. But nevertheless, Christian Science and theta consciousness are essentially one and the same thing, because both systems allow direct access to God and all the attributes of all the divinity attached thereto. Now the question remained, would James and Ann ever convince any of their Christian Science friends of this realization?

CHAPTER 41

There was an expression of one of James' friends that James was always "muddying the waters" with the new things he and Ann learned and experienced. James would always respond, "The more we learn the less the water is muddied and the clearer it becomes. That is why Ann and I are so fanatical about our studies and practices. The more we learn, the better our lives become as things appear clearer and make more sense. No one can actually countermand this statement or disprove it. What we are learning people may not like, but that it is extremely enlightening is undeniable."

A case in point about this was James' studying of *The Keys of Enoch*, by Dr. J. J. Hurtak. James would study this book for a period of time and then put it aside to digest what he had just read. Then he would read some more and repeat the process. As this continued over many cycles, each time James found things he had not seen or previously understood, and new information and understanding were attracted and assimilated into his life.

This recurring process of his study of *The Keys of Enoch* was quite amazing to James. It became progressively clearer to James there was an immense presence controlling things on Earth, the solar system, and the galaxy and the entire universe. Some people called this "intelligent design," but James referred to it as "a controlling intelligence." It likewise became more apparent to him there were specific codes and templates of light and sound that were the foundation of creation, which resided on the atomic level of creation and then established at higher levels of creation manifested in people, plants, planets, solar systems and galaxies. These atomic codes could be computer language... or at least James leaned in this direction, especially in light of the fact that Dr. Hurtak asserted there was a huge computer in the center of the Universe, which he believed stored all information from all galaxies and civilizations.

Also, James had read Dr. Hubert Yockey's book, *Information Theory, Evolution, and the Origins of Man,* which clearly revealed how human DNA was a binary pairs computer code. Additionally, James read where Bill Gates said that DNA was a binary pairs computer code that was vastly more complicated than any computer code ever written by Microsoft Corp. So James began to realize these binary pairs computer codes could quite possibly apply to all types of living; even non-organic forms!

Soon after, James found information that activating the telomerase strands at the end of it, through the use of Sanskrit mantras, chanting and prayer, could even reprogram DNA! But he sure did meet with unanimous resistance to the concept of reprogramming or changing DNA! There were many experts in genetics who were sure once you received your personal DNA codes; you were basically stuck with them—for better or worse! Yet James had annotated proof of the power of the Sanskrit mantra, "Gayatri," wherein people were healed of serious sickness, disease, and emotional trauma. Scientist's had actually measured a chemical change occurring at the end of telomerase strands. James had learned from reading the *Kauai Hindu Monastery Newsletter* DNA was reprogrammed through some type of undetermined process.

There were also many other forces and sources which were factors in James and Ann's life that kept things constantly interesting and fascinating. Their friend, Sue, funneled them information from several sources that would even more radically improve their lives. The first of which was from the Kabbalah Center: *The 72 Names of God* from Exodus 14, verses 19-21. These names were basically unknown to Christians because they were in the Torah, not the Bible, and obviously delineated in Hebrew.

Regardless of this paradox, James and Ann studied the names every day; James especially was quite enthralled with the names of God since he felt they were literally a map of creation and the perfect templates or forms, which were part of our essential Earth history and traditions; this wealth of knowledge was obscured right now and remained so for centuries and most likely, millennia.

So James started to see non-sequential patterns, which appeared to him and provided new and clearer meaning to the names and the utilitarian aspects that made the names applicable to daily life. What James learned studying the "72 Names," reading the lines from right to left, unlike English, was very enlightening. In the non-sequential patterns, starting near the bottom of the diagram and working upward through the lines of various specific names and onward to the top line, which was a formula for mental healing of all disease, James discovered a functional clarity regarding the basis of all creation and existence. The top line of "The 72 Names of God" appeared extremely similar to a formula that was used in the Christian Science mental healing system. This made

James realize that he had found a very deep level, probably an essential level of "The Hidden Codes of God" which could be foundational for everything else he experienced in life!

The hidden code formula James uncovered consisted of starting at one name at the next to last line: "Hey Resh Chet" (connecting to the light), followed to a name on the third from bottom line, "Ayin Resh Yod" (the certainty that God is always there for us), followed by a name on the fourth to bottom line, "Resh Hey Ayin" (finding the good in the bad), to a name of the middle line, "Aleph Nun Yod" (seeing the big picture), to another name on the middle line, "Mem Nun Daled (overcoming fears), to another name on the fourth line from the bottom "Vav Vav Lamed" (making the impossible possible), going back up to the middle line, "Yod Chet Vav" (removing obstacles) and then up to the first line.

James moved sequentially with eight names on the top line, from the right to the left: "Vav Hey Vav (fixing the past and creating happiness), "Yod Lamed Yod (boosting our energy), "Samesh Yod Tet" (creates miracles), "Ayin Lamed Mem" (eliminates negative thoughts), "Mem Hey Shin" (leads to healing), "Lamed, Lamed, Hey" (understanding subconscious messages), "Aleph Kaf Aleph" (restores things to their perfect state), "Kaf Hey Tav" (defuses negative energy and stress).

Once finally linked together, James realized how things fit together and revealed the bigger picture of creation and existence and it flowed like this: As we connect to the light/God, we have the certainty and knowledge that God is *always* there for us, which allows us to find good in the bad, and allows us to see the bigger picture, which allows us to *overcome* our fears, and makes the impossible possible...

242

which in the greater cycle of things removes obstacles. Thus, James centered on the prelude... the foundation for a formula for mental healing that follows.

As we fix the past and our happiness ensues, our energy is boosted, which puts us in a state of consciousness to create miracles, and from that mental and emotional position of creation, all our negative thoughts are removed, which opens us to a condition of healing. This healing is aided by understanding subconscious and restores things to a natural, perfect state and eradicates negative energy and stress.

James started using this protocol on his patients and noticed virtually miraculous healing results in most cases, but not all. From this, James realized that some conditions could take multiple treatments to get the desired results, just as in similar Christian Science treatments. He felt very comfortable with this protocol because it was so similar to Christian Science healing treatments, even though the terminology was different. The way "The 72 Names of God" corresponded with both Christian Science and the lucid daydream protocols espoused and used by the great Greek healer, Asclepius, was a triple cross validation of the three approaches and the validity in all of them. James was ecstatic at this overlapping cross verification.

Beyond this, there was a corresponding verification from the research of Louise L. Hay and her book, *You Can Heal Your Life,* which showed how the negative emotions: fear, anger, resentment and depression, could be viewed as the fundamental causes of sickness and disease and their positive counterparts: humor, laughing, joy and gratitude, as powerful palliative and "medicine" for any healing situation. Hays' work also fit perfectly within "The Hidden Codes of God,"

243

and James was blown away that these four "Hidden Codes of God" proved the same point, and that point was: *Any and all conditions of disease, sickness and even death—yes, the purported inevitability of death—could be transcended without medicine or surgery!*

So as James studied and pondered how all these things fit together so nicely, he marveled how nicely self-healing through subconscious messages meshed with Asclepius' lucid daydreaming healing. James used something similar to this formula for Christian Science healing four decades previously and was further elated how overcoming fears and eliminating negative thoughts, almost literally emanate from Mary Baker Eddy's, *Science and Health with Key to the Scriptures.*

Also, James also focused on "Samesh Aleph Daled" (the power of prosperity) from "The 72 Names of God." It was only after repeating the name hundreds, or perhaps thousands of times, that James realized that "Samesh Aleph Daled" would not have been in the "72 Names" unless it was an inherent right of all humans on Earth to be prosperous and flourish. Certainly, this belief was counter to the prevailing belief that there was only a certain amount of good jobs and a limited amount of resources, and only a few people could be prosperous. Yet this important phrase gave James an implicit verification that there was in fact enough abundance from the original templates of creation by God, that there could be prosperity for all peoples.

That belief would be cross-validated by the next thing in which James and Ann became interested. But "Aleph Kaf Aleph," also enthralled James; it was from the names of God, and it implied an already inherent perfection in the creation and order of all things. So this meant that things already being perfect did not have be created from scratch or recreated! He

244

embraced how it fit perfectly into the concepts in *Science and Health...* wherein Mary Baker Eddy also revealed that man was created in the perfect image and likeness of God. And this, too, could be framed within the concepts of *The Keys of Enoch.* There was a real meshing of things here that would be further validated by *The Emerald Tablets* of Hermes Trismegistus, and *The Pattern on the Trestleboard,* a series of fundamental truths used for understanding the "nature of reality" and understanding the nature of ourselves.

James mind continued to spin and he also became intrigued with the name of God, "Aleph Lamed Daled," which denoted "overcoming the evil eye." James and Ann could see this was important in the light of what they learned from *Science and Health...* where Mrs. Eddy was adamant every Christian Scientist should protect them from "aggressive mental suggestion." While Mrs. Eddy never quite completely defined what "aggressive mental suggestion" was, James and Ann assumed it was the malevolent thoughts of other people, akin to Voodoo... but not necessarily limited thereto.

In fact, James had been accused by people whom he had become disappointed in with their statements and actions, for mentally assaulting them with his upset and angry thoughts! And likewise, he had felt the wrath of other people's unkind thoughts. So both James and Ann found reciting the phrase, "Aleph Lamed Daled," would meet the behests of Mary Baker Eddy daily and throughout the day, serve to protect themselves from the damaging negative and malevolent thoughts of not only people but organizations, governments and the narrow perspectives of many religions that emanated from religious zealots who had no tolerance for anything that did not conform with their dogma.

Always thinking, James wondered how this would be effective in protection from radionics and HARP attacks directed by governments and organizations. He had already endured the radionic attack many years ago where Damien broadcast vibrations at James, not in order to attempt to heal him, but to use the frequencies, as Lynn's ex-boyfriend, to harm someone new in her life. James had also studied the writings of Dr. Nick Begich, who had accumulated a lot of research and information about how HAARP signals, which are an extra low frequency (ELF) whereby people can be brainwashed and even made sick and possibly even killed. Both the HAARP and radionic devices use transmitting frequencies to modify or change things or the properties related thereto.

So the question for James and Ann was, "How could repeating a simple phrase protect you from the thoughts of a person or devices which emit radio frequencies?" The answer to this came to them from a rather interesting front: their understanding that the language, Hebrew, was considered a sacred language, as well as Sanskrit. This sacredness resulted from sounds that emanated from speaking these languages, which created healing and protective vibrations, the result of their connection to the higher aspects of the Divine/God.

For James and Ann, this was more understandable when viewed within the perspective that most versions of the creation of the world referred to God uttering words, whose essence was vibration and the actions of phonons, which are aspects of atoms. James remembered the phrase from Genesis of the "Holy Bible" and "The Torah" which referred to how things were created where it said, "And the word was God and the word was with God." This then would indicate that words and their corresponding vibrations were capable of creating and manifesting things, including all aspects of creation.

Essentially, James realized the actual mechanics of this supported that the higher aspects of the words, "Aleph Kaf Aleph (restoring things to their perfect state) would cancel and/or destroy any negativity such as anger or malice, or any other lower vibration. James thought a comparison to this would be in the concept of "noise cancellation technology," where a noise could be lessened or eliminated by producing the corresponding opposite noise… basically a sound wave eliminated by a counter-wave. And so the vibration of the Hebrew letters worked in a similar manner, to cancel out or eliminate negativity, sickness and poverty. Once again, embracing their many previous revelations, James and Ann knew they had stumbled onto more of "the Hidden Codes of God."

The couple also began studying two disciplines from the Builders of the Adytum (BOTA), which was founded by Dr. Paul Foster Case, whose background was in the Golden Dawn Order of Rosicrucian's. As with other valuable information, Sue provided these resources, and ringing so true and powerful to James and Ann, fit nicely in synch with the other "Hidden Codes of God."

The first concept from Dr. Case's BOTA organization James and Ann studied was *The Emerald Tablets* of Hermes Trismegistus, also known as the "Smagardine Tablets." The tablets were translated by Dr. Case, Sir Isaac Newton and The Phoenician, among others, but Dr. Case's translation had such a beautiful flow to it that it stood above the other translations, including that of Sir Isaac Newton, who James venerated not only for his knowledge of physics and mathematics, but also for his spiritual insights.

Anyway, getting back to Hermes, James believed he could well have been of extraterrestrial origin. Hermes was his name in ancient Greece and he was considered a god in Greek mythology, which might have been more fact than myth. And before Greece, Hermes was known as Thoth, a netter god who would be considered as a person that was between the populace of ancient Egypt and the ultimate one and only God. Thus Thoth was a great, exalted teacher for whom there are still references to in Egypt. Additionally, Dr. Hurtak, in *The Keys of Enoch*, attributed Hermes as also being Enoch, which once again put Hermes in rather illustrious company on the Kabbalistic "Tree of Life" and at an extremely high level therein. So from this perspective, James and Ann already had the highest regard for Hermes!

Their study revealed "The Emerald Tablets" consisted of two paragraphs of powerfully distilled information as follows:

"True without falsehood, certain and most true, that which is above is that which is below and that which is below is that which is above, for the performance of the miracles of the One Thing. And as all things are from One, by the mediation of One, so all things have their birth from this One Thing by adaptation. The Sun is the father, the Moon is the mother, and the Wind carries it in its belly, its nurse the Earth. This is the father of all perfection or consummation of the whole world. Its power is integrating, if it be turned into Earth.

Thou shall separate the earth from the fire, the subtle from the gross, suavely and with great ingenuity. It ascends from earth to heaven and descends again to earth, and receives the power of the superior and of the inferiors. So thou hast the glory of the whole world, therefore let all obscurity flee before thee. This is the strong force of all forces overcoming every subtle and penetrating every solid thing. So the world was created. Hence were all wonderful adaptations of which this is the manner. Therefore, I am called Hermes Trismegistus, having the three parts of the philosophy of the whole world. What I have to tell is completed concerning the Operation of the Sun."

James was filled with delight because, once again, the hidden code cross-validated the other beliefs to which he and Ann had been exposed and it was scientifically accurate and yet distilled into easy-to-understand paragraphs. These two paragraphs indicated there was a direct interrelationship between Heaven and Earth and vice versa, and that miracles that existed at one of these places also existed at the other place, simultaneously. There was further revelation that all types of creation come from the One or the Creator and that the Sun, which is a symbol of God, rules over everything. And there was a declaration: *Perfection is the essence of everything, and literally consumes the Earth and can be integrated through it.*

James' next revelation was that man does have the power to transcend the limitations of the Earth through the power of fire, which is symbolic for cleansing and highly energizing. And since man is surrounded by the power and glory of the Creator, there is nothing he cannot understand and master. God's power is so pervasive and extends to all of his creation, not only man, but literally pervades and penetrates and infuses all things, regardless of their substance or composition.

James took some time for quiet repose; he was starting to realize there was a common energy that infused all things. He remembered Mrs. Eddy writing in *Science and Health with*

Key to the Scriptures that God was omnipresent, omniscient and omnipotent and that everything was comprised of Spirit. Translated, this meant that God was everywhere, all knowing and all power purveyed by Spirit, which is basically electromagnetic energy. The only thing James could see that would allow God to express all of these attributes was through the vast sea of atoms, which are electromagnetic in essence, and which collectively become atomic force and scientifically known as the building blocks or substance of everything.

Yet Mrs. Eddy stated clearly that the world is not controlled by atomic force. But in his heart James was confident that if Mrs. Eddy had discovered what he had uncovered, she would be able to accept his conclusion. Her book was written, after all, in the later 1800's, when physicists thought that atoms were dense matter; however, today, even though this belief is still prevalent, all of the data and research actually indicate atoms are only energy. Regardless of this, there were more and more texts that implied there was a God who was expressed in a strong field of energy and that God was the source thereof!

James and Ann next tackled the study of another BOTA source, *The Patterns on the Trestleboard: This is Truth About the Self,* written by Dr. Paul Foster Case, and another gift from Sue. *The Patterns on the Trestleboard* consisted of eleven distilled statements that Dr. Case had learned in the Golden Dawn Rosicrucian organization. The statements begin with relating how all the power of the Universe is here and now, and that we are expressions of good through God who is the creational and sustaining force of all things. The document then relates how there is a "Limitless Substance" that meets all our needs be they spiritual or for survival. *The Patterns on the Trestleboard* further say there is an undeviating Justice that operates in all of our lives and that there is a beauty in all forms of creation, regardless of size and stature. It further reveals that there is an unending source of wisdom that allows us to understand all things and that there is a splendorous, unlimited field of light. The final message is that our lives are based upon "Eternal Being" and that Spirit penetrates our flesh.

James could not have been more elated when he feasted his eyes on *The Patterns on the Trestleboard* because once again, this was even further cross-validation of not only an emerging pattern, but also much to James' delight, the undeniable synchronicity in the concepts from different sources that re-appeared with a stunning regularity. James was stunned! *Here are "Hidden Codes of God" of which more than ninety nine percent of humanity is completely unaware!* James was so impressed because he believed he recognized the keys to the un-enslavement and the ensuing liberation and a more even distribution of wealth and power and dignity that come there from, but his heart was exploding as he thought, *And most magnificent of all… the complete delineation of our relationship with our Creator*

With the introduction to *The Patterns on the Trestleboard* there was once again overlapping validation with: *The 72 Names of God, Science and Health with Key to the Scriptures, The Emerald Tablets* of Hermes, *The Patterns on the Trestleboard* and the *Keys of Enoch*, which when combined created a greater sum of value and understanding than when they were viewed separately; the compounding factor was clearly evident to James. Interestingly enough, James and Ann would compound and combine even, in short order!

It seemed to James and Ann that Jesus (Yeshuya) would have been familiar with most of the things they studied, including *The Emerald Tablets*, but not necessarily *The Patterns on the Trestleboard*. It had been conjectured by some biblical scholars that Jesus could have been well versed in the knowledge of the Kabbalah. But James and Ann remembered the New Testament account of how Jesus amazed the Rabbi's with his vast knowledge and understanding of scripture at twelve years of age. So the Rabboni (Rabbi), Jesus/Yeshuya could certainly have given an exception to the forty year old rule regarding studying of the Kabbalah, which is known to represent a distinctively Jewish approach intimately bound to the Scriptures; he just as easily could have assimilated the *Book of Enoch*, and for that matter, Hermes! Could Jesus have been instructed in the Indian Sanskrit texts and the Tibetan knowledge? James further pondered the implication of certain sources of information in India and Tibet, which were derived from an oral tradition, and certainly indicated this was possible!

| CHAPTER 42

James and Ann had been studying Kriya Kundalini Yoga for a long period of time and lately had begun the study of ancillary texts related thereto. One text they studied was *Thirumandiram*; considered by Avatar, Satguru, and Kriya Yoga Siddha and Thirumoolar, as somewhat a final authority on subtle matters of philosophy and theology. The book had finally been translated from Sanskrit and there were verses contained therein that usually contained several lines of text—essentially a poetry of sorts. The information contained in this book was a map to attain enlightenment and immortality of the human body.

The verse in *Thirumandiram* that stood out to James and Ann was the verse that states, "There is but one God and Nandi is his name." Since Ann knew that Nandi, a cow, was representative of Shiva (God), she felt this was irrefutable proof Hinduism was not a polytheistic religion of many Gods, as had been so widely promulgated and proliferated, especially by Christians. Actually, James and Ann had been pondering this concept a long time before they unveiled the knowledge in *Thirumandiram*. They both had often talked to others who brought up this purported polytheistic concept to denigrate Hinduism, and sometimes even the practice of Yoga; it was a distortion that the many so-called Gods such as Ganesh, Lakshmi, and Durga among others, were actually a fine detailing of the many attributes and qualities of God.

As well as their study of *Thirumandiram,* James and Ann also delved into "The Yoga Sutras," by Kriya Yoga Siddha-Patanjali, who was also an Avatar and Satguru. The Satguru part meant that Patanjali was beyond a mere Guru. So it gave him venerated status between Yogi's and Hindus... and James and Ann. Patanjali talked about Yoga being a cleansing process when he stated, "Yoga is the process of cleansing the subconscious mind." This was also the process James and Ann went through as they were exposed to the various aspects of "The Hidden Codes of God," which allowed them to reframe things in their minds. But each was sensitive to the feeling there was something vastly more significant than this revelation.

In "The Yoga Sutras," Patanjali discussed overcoming the state of death, revealing how it could be accomplished by mastering Satyama or Kriya Dhyana and Samdhi, which comprises Kriya Dhyana and Dhāraṇā, and Kriya Kundalini Pranayam, and allows access to Samadhi. This was exactly what they both had practiced for many years after Yogi Govindan Satchidanada taught it to them. James had become obsessed with the practice of Kriya Kundalini Pranayam and it easily allowed him to spend hours at a time in Samadhi, a breathless state of ecstasy.

Samadhi is a special state of bliss and euphoria that can be achieved while a person's breath and heart beat either cease completely or only randomly occur and at largely spaced intervals. As significant as this is, especially the cessation of breathing, which after four minutes was believed to cause significant brain damage by virtually all medical experts, the reverse actually happened—James' consciousness and his understanding of things was vastly increased. It was possible for him to receive information about things that were not contained in any books extant on Earth. Patanjali called this ability "celestial knowledge" and the Indian Vedas and Upanishads, which were ancient scriptures, termed it "Akashic knowledge." Distilled, both of them relate to heavenly or divine knowledge.

Needless to say, this opened a whole new "can of worms" for James and Ann because far too many people believed Divine knowledge was beyond the purview of mere mortals, effectively leaving us blocked and separated from our Creator! Yet, Mary Baker Eddy, in *Science and Health...* extensively discussed how all intelligence comes from God and not a brain. She often wrote of how Divine Mind was the only intelligence in the Universe, which is correlative to Patanjali and the ancient Indian Sanskrit texts. Even "the sleeping prophet," Edgar Cayce, brought through volumes of information about scientific, medical and anthropological concepts, which were unknown at their time of revelation, yet subsequently were validated and confirmed by scientific studies. In fact, James and Ann constantly utilized their "Akashic or celestial connection" to gain insights and knowledge into new concepts and determine whether information they encountered had substantial validity.

Still another Indian text James and Ann studied was *The Bhagavad Gita*, which was about the experiences of Krishna and Arjuna. Krishna was a son of Shiva/God, as was Jesus/Yeshua, a Son of God. There was a great amount of wisdom and information expounded upon in this book and on page 369 of the Paramahansa Yogananda translation; Krishna related what happens in the breathing process when prana is breathed into the body. Therein, it is explained:

...Fire and light, Yagna and Agna and sound, vibration and the holy sound "Aum" are concentrated into the body and the more of this prana that is breathed in, the more the body resembles energy and the less it resembles a dense material form.

The additional knowledge thoroughly excited James; it showed a practical effect of Kriya Kundalini Yoga that had never been explained to him. It spurred him to be more dedicated to his practice of Kriya Kundalini Pranayam and Samadhi because he now more fully understood the process and results of what he had been practicing. James further realized the body could be better nourished with Prana than by food, and researched the subject of Breatharianism, which promoted living without eating food.

In quite, uncommon hours, James became conscious he was not breathing for long periods of time during the day, even when he was working or studying, and sometimes even while dancing and walking for extended periods of time. With this realization James considered, *Was all the information about bodily nutrition, and brain damage due to the lack of breathing and oxygen, dispensed to subjugate peoples to religious, governmental and corporate control?* It was not difficult for him to embrace the possibility of control being very insidiously promulgated by the following dictum: *If you do not buy our food and medicine, you will degenerate and die.* And yet James saw how that particular concept created an unending class of consumers, which would need to purchase or barter for those things.

And even worse, there were mountains of information accruing that showed that eating genetically modified food (GMO's) was not only eliminating bio-diversity, but also provided people with foods they could not properly digest and might even be allergic to. James also deliberated on a monopoly of the supply of seeds created by Monsanto and its subsidiary, Pioneer Seeds, over the supply and availability of seeds to grow a wide array of crops. There was significant evidence GMO crops were toxic to honeybees, which are essential to pollinating open pollinated crops—those that have not been genetically modified. In effect, ensuring a pollination mechanism was no longer a viable alternative, and with honeybees no longer spreading pollen to open pollinated crops, farmers would not be able to produce food, as was previously possible. The end result: Pioneer Seeds would be the sole source supplier of crop seeds; effectively creating a monopoly, coincident with no competition and higher prices paid by consumers to this monopoly.

A similar environment was created for allopathic medicines, through the prevailing system of delivering medical care. The *Physician's Desk Reference* (PDR) clearly indicated that even simple over the counter pain relief medications could have many deleterious effects upon the body. In fact there were so many anecdotal experiences of doctors prescribing medication of which they were not even aware of the side effects. Another big question welled in in James' mind, *Do they not care solely because they get extravagant paid vacations at exotic locales, just to come and listen to the benefits of a new drug for an hour or two and then play golf for the balance of the paid-for vacation?*

By the time James explored Breathairianism concepts he was already pre-primed to understand living without eating food because of the insights that he had received from the *Bhagavad Gita* and other Yogic texts. He easily digested these concepts because of the evidence he had accumulated that the body was better nourished by Prana/the electromagnetic life force than by food. Also, there was the idea that some people considered the amount of energy necessary to digest food exceeded the amount energy that was derived there from. The concept could be deemed factually accurate, simply by reframing things and not assume the human body was only nourished by eating food and the digestion thereof. This was not difficult for James as he had the pictures of the auric/pranic fields of electromagnetic energy that surrounded not only the human body, but also all other living forms such as animals and plants.

James knew this energy field had been irrefutably proven to exist by Kirilian photography and magnetic field photography. If something no longer has the force of life within it, the Kirilian and magnetic fields of energy will no longer surround them. But if something is still living and a part of it is removed, such as part of a leaf from a plant or part of a limb from a human body, the energy field of the missing part would still be apparent and visible. The facts may have astonished James had he not been learning the concepts of the "energy body."

So, because James could easily accept all of this, it was also easy to reach a conclusion few other people had, which was that the essence of the human body was energy—electromagnetic energy—that could be both viewed and measured by instruments, such as an electrometer or dowsing rod. James bounced his ideas off of Ann as he asked her, "Do you find this concept that every thing and object is energy, or is this way too bizarro and far-fetched?"

"You have already uncovered sufficient information to substantiate your points and concepts, so what you are

258

proposing is not only logical, but so correct." Ann declared. "The fact that your ideas will meet considerable resistance is irrelevant, but to those of us who have assiduously pursued this knowledge, which has been compounded, step by step, we seek to uncover more of the 'God Codes.' The only question here is how many people will pull themselves out of their comfort zones so that they can assimilate this liberating and truly revolutionary information."

"Yes," James replied, "I agree with everything you said and more, because for me I already exist better than before by eating significantly less food and probably drinking more water. And, I have noticed that for large parts of the day I am not breathing nor is my heart beating. This strongly indicates my body is more nourished by Prana, Chi, or life force rather than by breathing… and the ingestion and digestion of food. It is undeniably true there are nutrients in food but the prana/life force of this food may be significantly more nourishing than the other substances contained in the food, apart from the prana. Additionally, it is certainly true that oxygen has components that sustain life in the body but what if it's main purpose and importance is to transport Prana/life force throughout the body?"

James continued, "Yet in the Samdhi we have both experienced many times, where our breathing and heart rate have been suspended, we not only come back physically undamaged but enhanced by the insights into God and creation we bring back with us. Our brains and our consciousness are expanded and this truly contravenes what is believed to be possible; we should return from Samadhi with damaged brains and yet they are not adversely affected. It is so possible to exist without eating food; I am actually ashamed that I have not completely done so. Even a recent study published in *The Journal of Metabolic Sciences* revealed the discovery that at least 25% of the body's nourishment comes from outside the body!"

The trend was becoming too obvious to ignore. The evidence supported James and Ann's hunches and what they perceived was not only possible, but also ready to be realized by humanity at large once they had been exposed to "The Hidden Codes of God." An indispensible part of these hidden codes, which stimulated these hunches were contained in Kriya Kundalini Yoga and specifically the Pranayam breath meditation and the corresponding state of breathlessness experienced in samadhi—the state wherein James and Ann found their minds become still, and concentrated, and where the limits of the human mind are easily transcended.

James, more than Ann, often got frustrated by how people resisted the self-evident because it was too difficult for them to stretch themselves to accept new concepts. To James, it was all rather plain and simple, and the "prejudice filters" of people prevented them from evolving into something better than they already are. This pushed James to the brink of writing a book to explain the concepts; a book soon materialized.

CHAPTER 43

James and Ann ultimately assimilated so many of "The Hidden Codes of God," that Ann encouraged James to write their experiences as a published book. James agreed the need for this undertaking was self-evident. *The only way to liberate people from their ignorance and enslavement was to unveil all of this—to lift the curtain so the light can shine in*," James thought. *If Ann and I can be so changed by these keys, to living a radiant and satisfying life, that have been dispensed to us by 'The Hidden Codes of God,' everyone should likewise have the same opportunity. Of this I am most positive and certain.*"

So James started writing, bringing to fruition what he had envisioned earlier through, *A Map to Healing*, but he found out that Dr. Robert Newton, with whom he had written *Pathways to God*, was already beginning a book called, *A Map to Healing and Your Essential Divinity Through Theta Consciousness*. Since he knew Dr. Newton, from their previous association and working relationship, James decided to join forces and co-write the book as a ghostwriter. Rather than becoming famous, the important point to James was that the information was made readily available to the public realms and consciousness. What he originally contemplated was to expand the healing protocols of "Theta Healing" and dispense the ways in which the state of theta consciousness could be reliably experienced. He and Dr. Newton realized it was a rather puny scope for a book that needed more to be fully manifested and shared. Thus the scope of the book grew by leaps and bounds, and with each day of writing, the book was unveiled and progressed.

Interestingly, the book was written without any outline, unlike James and Dr. Newton's first book! Additionally, James and Dr. Newton wound up writing an introduction about ten times longer than either anticipated, but found it flowed almost effortlessly. James' experience was similar to his receiving information from the Akashic Records— celestial knowledge. It was on the same level, or perhaps more elevated, than the information from the Indian Vedas and Upanishads, and connecting to the level of "Divine Mind," such as was discussed by Mary Baker Eddy in *Science and Health....*"

The writers shared in their extensive introduction the belief that a foundation of perfection pervaded all creation on Earth and the entire Universe. With relative ease, it was achieved by relating the things that James and Ann and his other love interests and teachers had shared and uncovered, as well as knowledge culled by Dr. Newton. It included wisdom and knowledge from: *Science and Health with Key to the Scriptures*, *The Emerald Tablets* of Hermes Trismegistus, *The Pattern on the Trestleboard*, *The 72 Names of God* from Exodus, *The Yoga Sutras* and *The Bhagavad Gita*. It was natural draw on such a wide array of sources, making the introduction rather easy to compose.

The book exposed how we have been deliberately mis-programmed, including accepting mediocrity, lack of resources and hierarchical structures that favor a few people. The pages revealed how this programming has been promulgated through our educational system, corporate structure, governmental systems and many of our religions.

This less than optimal programming, as explained in the manuscript, was the cause of all of our personal and world problems. The authors disclosed their belief of how we have been erringly led to believe there are limited resources, that only a small amount of people can be successful among the populace, there is only just so much money and wealth that can be shared among the populace, and how each person must accept their plight in life without complaining.

James and Dr. Newton wrote about the incompetence of the existing system of delivering health care and the inherent dangers of the drugs and surgeries that it dispenses. They also documented "false flag operations" that are undertaken by extra governmental sources and then blamed on innocent parties, such as the 9-11 debacle and the myth about jet fuel causing structural steel to melt in the Trade Towers, which is physically impossible, in the opinion of many competent structural engineers and architects! It was also pointed out how Tower Seven collapsed without ever being stricken by a plane and how obviously the building had to have been taken down by a controlled demolition, which included Towers One and Two, since all these buildings pan-caked instead of falling to the side.

A wealth of information was found in the introduction, and James and Dr. Newton had not yet given credit to all those people who were their teachers and made the book possible. *A Map to Healing and Your Essential Divinity Through Theta Consciousness* literally teemed with "The Hidden Codes of God," which James and Ann had accumulated and practiced over the years.

The book contained further discussion of how our Federal Reserve banking system is not in fact a federal bank, but actually a highly privatized entity that only serves the interests of the very few ultra rich and privileged, elite individuals and their ultra secret assemblages. In essence, James and Dr. Newton revealed that our money system, based on nothing of inherent value such as gold or silver, is a fractionalized or vapor currency and an elaborate Ponzi scheme, to wit. Additionally, attention was drawn to how the action of charging interest on money created out of thin air is disingenuous and sucks vitality from the economy and makes it inherently difficult for most business owners to acquire venture and expansion capital. Leaving no stone unturned, the writers explained their belief that the IRS is nothing more than a collection agency for the Federal Reserve Bank. They postured, "Why should a private bank should be the recipient of these revenues instead of the US government, itself?"

James and Dr. Newton also discussed the endless parade of choreographed wars, which promised to liberate people of various countries, but only seemed to destabilize and impoverish the people. And they wrote about the collateral damage to the civilians of these countries and the massive injuries and death of our own soldiers. James revealed how easy it is for the controlling elite to create false scenarios to justify these wars to "protect us," when in reality it is believed the wars are only to protect their fat bank accounts, which are derived from the sales of munitions produced by the military industrial complex. James and Dr. Newton also questioned whether things such as the National Defense Authorization Act and The Patriot Act really were meant to protect us from outside threats or rather to control and survey the populace of the USA.

Ultimately… in the meat of the book in Chapter One, James and Dr. Newton gave detailed information of the inherent perfection of our Earth and the entire Universe from the many ancient texts they had studied and the supporting scientific proof of this perfection. For the scientific proof, James and Dr. Newton relied upon Valery P. Kondratov's *Geometry of a Uniform Field*, which showed recurring forms of geometric shapes occurring on the atomic level of creation. They opened readers to Dr. Hugh Ross' work in astrophysics, which showed perfectly planned creational schemes executed within very tight parameters, regarding strong nuclear force and electromagnetism. The co-authors also used Dr. Ross' work to prove beyond a doubt that there was a precise controlling intelligence controlling the Earth and the Universe—be it Creator, God, or whatever!

In Chapter Two, James and Dr. Newton talked about how medicines and herbs really heal, which is essentially from the vibratory energy that causes a shift in consciousness. Additionally they wrote about the superiority of energy such as acupuncture, magnetic healing, and mental healing including Christian Science and Theta Healing and Theta Consciousness Healing. The authors wrote about the futility and danger of trying to cure cancer with oncology protocols, even showing how chemotherapy basically used a formula similar to mustard gas, an extremely debilitating chemical agent used in World War I and then banned by the Geneva Conventions. James followed that information with a list of at least ten alternative protocols for healing cancer, which are known to be efficient and cost effective, unlike oncology treatments.

In Chapter Three, James and Dr. Newton talked about the many ways to entrain consciousness at the level of theta/divinity. These included: "Backflow Meditation," Tai Chi "Standing Meditation," Kriya Kundalini "Pranayam," and certain types of music, dancing, extreme sports and running. The chapter also included Sanskrit mantras and chanting and toning, followed by James and Dr. Newton carefully detailing how sexuality, practiced within the energy parameters they had learned, could also powerfully entrain consciousness in theta level/divinity. They even revealed how it was possible to have an orgasm without genital penetration!

In Chapter Four, James and Dr. Newton revealed an improved version of Theta Healing, which they labeled "Theta Consciousness Reprogramming and Healing." They explained how to entrain consciousness at theta level and detailed a protocol for mental healing of any and all situations and diseases. James and Dr. Newton provided support of how it all fit in with Christian Science healing and how both disciplines were complimentary.

In Chapter Five, James and Dr. Newton assiduously detailed how the essence of man and creation energy rather than material. To accomplish the detail, the writers relied on ancient and modern texts and the latest discoveries from physics, quantum physics and quantum mechanics. They used the treatises from Valery P. Kondratov and physicist Jay Lakshani, and added helium ion microscope pictures of a platinum crystal by Dr. Edwin Mueller, to illustrate the concepts. James and Dr. Newton also discussed how the energy from the center of "The Milky Way Galaxy" is more powerfully entering the Earth as per the research of Richard Hoagland and Dr. Hurtak in *The Keys of Enoch*.

James and Dr. Newton discussed how these energies blended with a higher consciousness entrained in theta trance/divinity level and from the understanding provided by: *Science and Health with Key to the Scriptures, The 72 Names of God* from Exodus, *The Pattern on the Trestleboard, The Emerald Tablets* of Hermes Trismegistus, *The Yoga Sutras,* and the *Bhagavad Gita.* The writers believed the practices could literally allow a person to transcend the death of the so-called material body and live in an energy body or body of light or a "garment of light" as discussed in ancient Gnostic texts. James and Dr. Newton shared with readers just how all of these things were basically like chemicals and their catalysts. The "chemicals" so noted are Kriya Kundalini Pranayam, the Tai Chi, "Standing Meditation," "The Backflow Meditation" and Sanskrit mantras as per the Gayatri Mantra.

The chapter noted the mahamrityonjaya mantra created an alchemical reaction that would cause the "light body"/"spirit body" to be manifested and/or appear. James and Dr. Newton wrote about how catalysts such as Kriya Kundalini Pranayam were recognized as essential ingredients/catalysts that brought the "chemicals"/teaching sources, such as *The Emerald Tablets,* etc. to a state of being highly useful and able to be integrated into our daily lives!

James and Dr. Newton further discussed how Dr. Robert Becker, in *The Body Electric,* regenerated the limbs of Salamanders through electrical stimulation. And that the same thing should be possible in humans through such things as "Q Laser," the "AIM" Program, acupuncture, magnetic acupuncture, color therapy as per the Dinsbaugh protocols, sound technology as per the work of John Keely and "Sound Signature" protocols, Reiki, Kriya Kundalini Pranayam, the

Tai Chi "Standing Meditation" and Qui Gong, as well as by other types of electrical stimulation. James and Dr. Newton discussed the fact that the energy outline of a cut leaf from a plant or a missing limb from a body still appearing in a Kirlian photograph gave further evidence that limbs/and parts of leaves should be able to be regenerated.

Their co-authoring led to a deep discussion of how psychic abilities are significantly enhanced at the level of theta consciousness and healing abilities. They likewise discussed the functions of breathing and blood circulation being more a function of infusing the body with Prana/life force/God force; and of oxygen being a carrier agent for this function. These pieces of knowledge were delivered to James from the Akashic records, since such information was nowhere to be found on Earth.

In Chapter Six, James and Dr. Newton discussed creating the "Spiritual World Order" as opposed to "The New World Order" of oppression and constriction as envisioned by the Illuminati (New World Order types). Pages were filled with how this "Spiritual World Order" could be manifested if more of the populace became entrained in theta consciousness. The creators went on to endorse that this process would greatly aid us in facing natural disasters, extreme weather patterns, the flipping of the Earth's magnetic poles and possible famine.

All of the things James and Ann had unveiled from "The Hidden Codes of God" were listed as ways that humanity could restore things on earth to their perfect state or "Aleph Kaf Aleph," from "The 72 Names of God" from the Torah.

Additionally, James and Dr. Newton discussed how sin was nothing more than our being ignorant of our inherent perfection and how the concepts of sin and hell had been deliberately used to control the populace at large, keeping them disempowered and controllable. And the writers expressed their belief the perfection of atoms, and their being aggregated into the atomic field proved perfection pervades everything, since all objects are composed of atoms.

In Chapter Seven, James and Dr. Newton delved into how the immortal light body could be created on Earth and how it had already been done, not only by Jesus, but myriad Kriya Yoga Siddha's such as: Agastyar, Attis of Phrygia, Babaji Nagaraj, Ram, Boganathur, Dionysus, Kokanavar, Krishna, Mataji Mithras, Osiris, Valmiki Nogababa, Rama Devar, and Thirumoolar. Further, James and Dr. Newton shared Jesus' behest where he said, "Greater works than these shall ye do also," meaning that we could perform and exceed the works of Jesus, himself!

Anointing oils, which are considered longevity agents, were discussed and James related they could include Bindhu (a translucent blue substance), monatomic gold, Occinum Sanctum (Holy Basil), Aloe Vera, Hydrogen Peroxide and ATP (AdenoTrioPhosphate). The pages shared evidence that Mary Magdalene may have covered Jesus' body with anointing oil, following his death and subsequent resurrection, and included James' discussion of becoming an assiduous practitioner of Kriya Kundalini Yoga and Pranayam breathing, and how it would enable the possible activation of the body of light and energy.

In Chapter Eight, James and Dr. Newton shared how many possible psychic abilities are developed and enhanced by having consciousness entrained in alpha and theta functioning. Chapter Nine covered what happens when humans die, which was explained as an impossible scenario since our consciousness just transfers to another dimension, upon our so-called demise. The manuscript discussed that this non-death scenario is supported by the fact that we are comprised of atoms, which do not die and cannot be destroyed.

In Chapter Ten, James and Dr. Newton discussed where a person goes when they die and categorically revealed that it is impossible to go to Hell, which has never been astro-localized. They included passages that revealed there are many dimensions of reality, stacked within the same space, as per "String Theory" and "Membrane Theory," and discussed the belief that we keep reincarnating on Earth until we realize and demonstrate our essential divinity. The process of realizing our divinity would be greatly aided by the assiduous practice of Kriya Kundalini Yoga and especially Pranayam breathing, creating an alchemical transformation of the body. Again, James and Dr. Newton emphasized that since micro-creation, at the atomic level is perfect, the macro-creation we exist in must likewise remain in this perfect state of "Aleph Kaf Aleph," or restore things to their perfect state! Finally, they related how there is no need for anyone to go to Hell, and that heaven can be created on Earth, as claimed by Mary Baker Eddy.

Creating Chapter Eleven surprised even James, and considerably so. The surprise was not contained in the first part of the chapter that talked about the strong possibility of upcoming geomantic and weather disturbances because Sun influences most likely caused by more energy coming into the

Earth, from the center of the "Milky Way Galaxy." No! It was the part about Breathairianism that came out of the blue, as it were! James literally learned the information about living without eating as he was conveying it. Some of the information came from Akashic insights, and once again, James realized that Kriya Kundalini Yoga and its Pranayam breath would enable someone to more rapidly become a Breathairian. The writing contained several yogic sources that indicated the Pranayam breath electrified and energized the body and James shared how it would sustain the body better than food. So, essentially, the body can be nitrified with Prana/life force!

In Chapter Twelve, James and Dr. Newton wrote about where humans stood in the overall scheme of things, where they were placed under the plant kingdom and animals, and how it aroused a lot of controversy, especially among fundamentalist Christians, as if living without eating was not controversial! James spent a lot of time extolling the virtues of plants and trees and all the miraculous things they did to provide an environment in which we could thrive, but that the opposite was not necessarily true of humans, in that we have not properly taken care of the Earth and our stewardship has been lacking. Their message included a discussion of how having dominion over the Earth really meant stewardship and taking care of our world!

Chapter Thirteen was a summary of the book, while the Epilogue was a synopsis of the basic information and the scope of the manuscript. At the very end of the book, James shared many formulas he received via Akashic insights. Much like the breathairian information, the inclusion of the formulas surprised James; he had not contemplated publishing anything of that nature, and was amazed at what had been revealed to him.

Overall, James was quite satisfied by what had been revealed to him in his collaboration with Dr. Newton as they finalized the book. Ann helped them proofread it, which was a monumental task in and of itself. James already knew he was not a good proofreader since he learned to look at things with a soft focus, as a result of his instruction in Tai Chi. *A Map to Healing and Your Essential Divinity Through Theta Consciousness* was finally published, after the slow and arduous publishing process. Getting the publisher to work at a sustained speed, and within James and Dr. Newton's time frame, was a difficult task. With the book completed, they looked forward to sharing "The Hidden Codes of God" that James and Ann had uncovered and practiced to enrich their lives and consciousness! Were there further books to come from James? Certainly, there was a good possibility that more of "The Hidden Codes of God" would be revealed to James and Ann, if past experiences were any indication of the future! Did they believe this would happen?

ABOUT THE AUTHOR

Dr. Robert J. Newton has lived his life much in the manner he writes... with a quest to surround himself with the highest level knowledge in the myriad areas that ensure we live rich, full lives. His education has been extensive, ranging from Speech and English at Cal State Fullerton, to a Juris Doctorate from American College of Law, and many certifications in alternative healing. He formalized his career in Naturopathic Medicine as a graduate of Clayton School of Natural Healing.

Newton has lived to serve others; operating an award-winning landscape and design company for many years, as a Christian Science healer for two decades, and more recently as an author, speaker and life and relationship coach. Yoga, Metaphysics, Spiritual Sciences, Natural Healing, World Religions, Ancient Hermetic teachings... this philosopher and champion for the world has tapped into the roots of spirituality, sexuality, life and love—all with the purpose to enlighten those with a common desire to utilize multiple methods and strategies to approach life more effectively, creatively, radiantly and with great abundance.

אבא

Thank you for reading *The Hidden Codes of God!*

Gaining exposure as an independent author, I rely mostly on word-of-mouth, so if you have the time and inclination, please consider leaving a short review wherever you can.

http://amzn.to/1IBDKSb

Also available on Kindle

http://amzn.to/1H8uVyX

OTHER BOOKS BY THE AUTHOR:

Beyond the Mists of Time: When Trees Ruled the Earth And The State of Balance and Euphoria That Ensued There From

Dr. Robert Newton, J.D., N.D.

Dr. Robert Newton, J.D., N.D.

Dr. Robert Newton, J.D., N.D.